On a little tour in France.

American ~ *the*
beginning *e,*
and wrote
talks abou
the archite
the people
the way.

Brief encounters, close encounters, encounters of any kind with folk who live in another country excited the old explorers and excite us still. Discovering how people live – what similarities and differences govern their lives – brings our travels to life. Rather more literature is written about people than about scenery; quite a few people, as well as places, feature in this book.

What pleasure we have talking to the people who run the sites in these guides. The lady in Normandy who told us that her lack of any language save her native French didn't stop her putting the world to rights with her English-speaking visitors till the early hours. The Dutchman who loves sharing his little patch of the South with people on holiday. The English family in the Gers who do it all for fun and company, and the French lady in the Dordogne who's delighted to have learnt to play conkers.

It is impossible to take even the littlest tour in France without discovering wonderful places. Our human-scale campsites are there to help you do that; to take you under the skin and behind the scenes of this spectacular country. Beyond the great Euro-motorways, beyond the interchangeable airport lounges and the international playground resorts, is a France with flavour. Savour it slowly and at ground level, and the richness of it all is yours. Return from your tour full of things felt and smelt, discovered and learnt. And people met, and friends made.

Make sure you know the rules of the road in the country you're exploring.

French driving is lively. The French regard speed limits as personal challenges, road signs as advisory and traffic lights as optional. Nowhere in the world do small cars with small engines perform as they do here. It's not fun driving a large vehicle or towing in heavy traffic; unless you have nerves of steel avoid central Paris (and the Périphérique) if you can. Happily the motorways are of superb quality and are seldom busy, the main Route Nationale roads are good in most places and on minor roads you can travel for miles without meeting so much as a 2CV. Remember, though:

- the French drive on the right (for quite a lot of the time)
- always be prepared to give way to the right at junctions and intersections. On some quiet country roads you must even give way to a minor road crossing a major one from the right.
- have with you a warning triangle, a set of spare bulbs, a nationality sticker, your registration papers, details of your international insurance cover and your driving licence; this must be a full one, and you must be over 18
- children under ten must sit in the back and wear seat belts. Specially-adapted baby seats are allowed in the front
- traffic regulations are strictly enforced, with hefty, on-the-spot fines
- motorways are privately operated – tolls (payable in cash or by VISA/Carte Bleue) are high
- international breakdown cover is advisable
- 'wild camping' is not allowed

SPEED LIMITS vary according to the type of road and the weather:

Motorways:	130kph on dry roads, 110 if wet
Dual carriageways:	110kph dry, 100 wet
All other roads:	90kph dry, 80 wet
Built-up areas:	50kph dry, 40 wet.

SOME COMMONLY-ENCOUNTERED SIGNS:

RALENTIR	*SLOW DOWN*
PRIORITE A DROITE	*GIVE WAY TO TRAFFIC FROM RIGHT*
SENS UNIQUE	*ONE-WAY STREET*
DEVIATION	*DIVERSION*
SAUF RIVERAINS	*RESIDENTS ONLY*
STATIONNEMENT INTERDIT	*NO PARKING*
SERREZ A DROITE/GAUCHE	*KEEP RIGHT/LEFT*
CHAUSSEE DEFORMEE	*UNEVEN ROAD SURFACE*
ACCOTEMENTS NON STABILISES	*SOFT VERGES*
RAPPEL	*THE LAST INSTRUCTION STILL STANDS*

Real
Exploring
Using the Telephone in France

Phoning home or booking sites, you'll need to phone while you're in France. Real explorers who know this country of old will recall days when this was not for the faint-hearted; these days, France has one of the most sophisticated telecommunications systems in the world. Some simple tips to help you find your way round it:

MASTERING THE TECHNOLOGY

- you can use your mobile phone, if it's the right sort – check with your dealer that it is, and that your network has reciprocal arrangements with France. If you buy one just before you go, you may have to pay a substantial security deposit against the cost of calls – again, your dealer will tell you.
- phone boxes are easy to use. Some take coins (arm yourself with an assortment), others take phone cards. These are called Télécartes, and can be bought in post offices, tobacconists and other shops displaying the sign 'Télécartes en vente ici'; 50 units cost around 40F, 120 units around 98. Most phone boxes accept incoming calls; if you want someone to call you back, hunt for the number of the box, usually cunningly concealed in one of the corners of the instruction notice in the kiosk.
- you can phone from post offices, and pay for your call at the end, and from bars, hotels etc – although this is likely to be expensive.

GETTING THE RIGHT NUMBER

Phone numbers in France have changed recently; they now have ten digits, usually written as five lots of two. Should you  encounter an eight-digit number, you'll need to add the new code in front of it. It'll be 01/02/03/04 or 05, depending on the region – this little map should help you decide which. To dial a French number from France, simply dial these ten digits – no special rules for Paris any more.

The procedure for dialling an overseas number has changed too. Simply dial 00, followed by the country code – 0031 for Holland, 0045 for Denmark, 0044 for the United Kingdom, etc. Then dial the usual number, dropping the first zero.

EMERGENCY NUMBERS: POLICE 17
FIRE 18
AMBULANCE 15

Foreign Fields

Real *Exploring* Tourist Information

The Well-informed Traveller.

Wherever you want your little tour in France to take you, it helps to be well-informed. There's a French Tourist Office in the capital cities of most countries which will send you details of places/activities which interest you. Equally, you can contact the Regional Tourist Offices in France directly for more detailed information on particular areas – the numbers are given on this map.

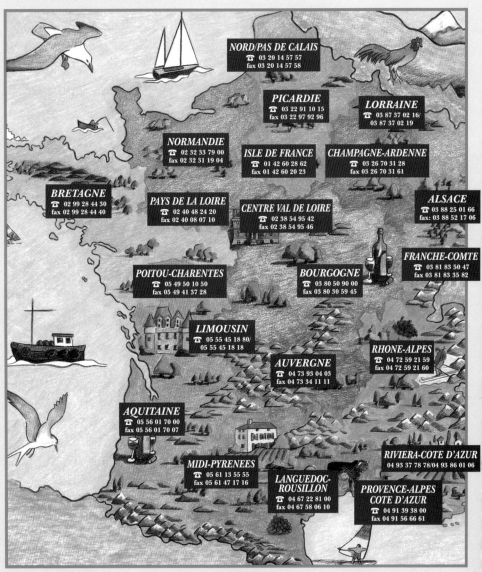

NORD/PAS DE CALAIS
☎ 03 20 14 57 57
fax 03 20 14 57 58

PICARDIE
☎ 03 22 91 10 15
fax 03 22 97 92 96

LORRAINE
☎ 03 87 37 02 16/
03 87 37 02 19

NORMANDIE
☎ 02 32 33 79 00
fax 02 32 31 19 04

ISLE DE FRANCE
☎ 01 42 60 28 62
fax 01 42 60 20 23

CHAMPAGNE-ARDENNE
☎ 03 26 70 31 28
fax 03 26 70 31 61

BRETAGNE
☎ 02 99 28 44 30
fax 02 99 28 44 40

PAYS DE LA LOIRE
☎ 02 40 48 24 20
fax 02 40 08 07 10

CENTRE VAL DE LOIRE
☎ 02 38 54 95 42
fax 02 38 54 95 46

ALSACE
☎ 03 88 25 01 66
fax: 03 88 52 17 06

FRANCHE-COMTE
☎ 03 81 83 50 47
fax 03 81 83 35 82

POITOU-CHARENTES
☎ 05 49 50 10 50
fax 05 49 41 37 28

BOURGOGNE
☎ 03 80 50 90 00
fax 03 80 30 59 45

LIMOUSIN
☎ 05 55 45 18 80/
05 55 45 18 18

AUVERGNE
☎ 04 73 93 04 03
fax 04 73 34 11 11

RHONE-ALPES
☎ 04 72 59 21 59
fax 04 72 59 21 60

AQUITAINE
☎ 05 56 01 70 00
fax 05 56 01 70 07

MIDI-PYRENEES
☎ 05 61 13 55 55
fax 05 61 47 17 16

LANGUEDOC-ROUSILLON
☎ 04 67 22 81 00
fax 04 67 58 06 10

RIVIERA-COTE D'AZUR
04 93 37 78 78/04 93 86 01 06

PROVENCE-ALPES COTE D'AZUR
☎ 04 91 39 38 00
fax 04 91 56 66 61

Preparing for trips is very much part of the fun. A well-mounted expedition creates comfort, minimises time-wasting and makes for voluptuous smugness.

Truly macho real explorers will of course protest here and mutter on about building a shelter for ten with two oak leaves and a sheepshank in the Boy Scouts. They have a point; travelling light can be intoxicating in the sense of freedom it brings. Witness though the other approach, the Doctor Livingstones and Hannibals, mounting their expeditions with enormous entourages, big budgets and odd definitions of essential. Happiness, surely, lies somewhere between the two.

A useful equipment checklist, for you to scorn or augment according to your style, follows shortly. First, though, you will need a tent, a caravan or a motor caravan, your own or hired, in order to carry your home on your back. (Usually at this point in these things snails get a mention, rather irrationally. You do NOT need something slow, aerodynamically disastrous and with – presumably – little storage space).

If you don't already own your equipment, you must decide which of these three options best suits you, your circumstances and your bank manager. This is a realm of irreconcilable camps and strong passions. Real explorers do it in tents, says one faction (prize, by the way, for the best printable suggestion for what follows 'Real Explorers do it .....' on the inevitable car sticker). Owners of towed caravans, and those of the self-propelled alternatives, smile gently at each other with an air of trying to humour the sadly misguided.

Not for us, but for the experts, to present the rival contestants!

Checklist

Bedding, linen, towels, tea towels, cloths
Crockery, cutlery, kitchen utensils, pots and pans
Food, cleaning materials, washing-up liquid, loo rolls
Rubbish bags, hose, garden furniture
Clothes, shoes, boots, waterproofs, toiletries
Prescriptions, drugs, medications, first aid supplies
Medical insurance/cover documents
Torch, penknife, string, matches, safety pins, superglue
Stationery, stamps
Books, magazines, music, games, toys, quizzes
Barbecue and equipment
Bikes, puncture repair outfit, tools
Maps, compass
Phonecard, small change or mobile phone
Vehicle documents, insurance details
Passports, tickets, travel documents

"Surely there is no better way for the intrepid traveller to explore Britain and beyond than from behind the wheel of a motorhome! Go where you want, when you want – all in 5-star luxury!

MARQUIS MOTORHOMES
Winchester Road
Lower Upham, nr
Southampton
Hampshire SO32 1HA
Tel: 01489 860 666
Fax: 01489 860 752

Even if you've never been in a motor caravan before, life behind the wheel of your mobile 'holiday home' couldn't be simpler. Power steering makes them easy to drive, and diesel engines make them economical. The luxurious interior puts most hotel rooms into the shade – and you can change the view from your window as often as you like!

Hiring is the ideal way to start. From April to October, you can hire one of our vehicles from our base near Southampton (or we can meet you at Heathrow or Gatwick airports). You must be between 23 and 70, be acceptable for insurance and hold a full driving licence. We take a lot of time and trouble showing you how to drive it, and how everything works inside.

You can hire by the week, or, if you have longer expeditions in mind, you can use our 'buy-back' scheme – a really economical proposition if your trip's going to take weeks or even months. Ask for our brochure for all the details.

Your vehicle comes equipped with everything you need, including cutlery, crockery, gas, maps etc – jump in and go! Even linen is available, and is provided free for overseas customers. (And if you get hooked and decide to buy within a year, we'll deduct the price of a week's hire from the price of your vehicle – we're leaders in sales as well as hire).

We have three sizes of motor caravan on offer; a 5.25m four-berth, a 5.9m five-berth and a 7m six-berth. They're all less than a year old, and of superb quality.

Real explorers, look no further!"

EVERNDEN CYCLES

47 Maidstone Road, Paddock Wood, Kent TN12 6DG
Tel: 01892 832823. Fax: 01892 832931

"Go exploring by bike – or go exploring on four wheels, take your bike with you and use it to transform your holiday when you get there.'

Any bike can be fitted with racks and panniers, so that you can carry a full camping outfit with you – there are even special tents available with built-in bike sheds! Equally, bikes can be carried on most vehicles – on the roof, on the boot, on the tailgate or using a towbar rack. A caravan or motor caravan dealer will advise you.

Cycling is booming, with lots of people coming back to it who haven't cycled since schooldays. A wonderful choice of cycles is available, and prices are reasonable. Important, though, to choose the right type.

Kids are easy – mountain bikes are available everywhere, they're tough enough for the most enthusiastic rough-ground riding and they're fashionable. Adults may have, deep in the coalshed, an old 'town' bike. Best leave it there – these are too heavy for most country riding. Best ignore also the glamorous (drop handlebar) road tourers and racing bikes. Picture yourself leading the Tour de France if you will, but these thoroughbred mounts are expensive and a little fragile for careering around campsites.

The solution is the recently-developed, hybrid 'town and country' bike, hugely popular because it suits all purposes – we sell hundreds. It's a traditional large-wheeled bike with an upright riding position, yet much lighter than a town bike (which you'll appreciate when you're loading it onto a bike rack or carrying it across a stile!). With 18 or 21 gears, it has medium-width, rugged tyres, and is ideal for using round the town and for light off-road use – forest tracks, canal towpaths and the like. By far the best buy.

All sorts of accessories, special clothing (don't forget your helmet) and cycle route books exist now to make this a smashing leisure activity and one of the best ways imaginable of keeping fit. Much better than trudging over the Alps with elephants!"

Photos courtesy of Dawes Cycles Ltd.

Tourer Marketing Bureau

Brahm Building, Alma Road, Headingley, LEEDS LS6 2AH
Telephone: 0113 230 4000

'Hannibal should have got himself a touring caravan. Half a million Brits have, and it's the most popular form of holiday in Britain. Hook it up to your existing car (or elephant) and off you go. Arrive at your destination, unhook it and you've got your car to go wherever you will and your 'base' to return to – unbeatable flexibility.

It's not hugely expensive either. A very good second hand model with all mod cons – and they really are mod – can be bought for about £3,000 (and if you're on a tight budget you'll find older ones for much less than that). A brand new one will probably be between £8,000 and £20,000, depending on how big (and how glamorous) you want it to be.

And glamorous they certainly are – look at the 'interior' picture below. Hand-crafted furniture, interior sprung beds and superb upholstery make for a feeling of real luxury. Newcomers are often astonished to find central heating, hot water, showers, flush toilets, fridge-freezers and microwaves. Many people now use their caravans all the year round – if you enjoy being out and about whatever the weather, you have a really cosy home-from-home to use as a base.

Would-be touring caravan explorers should consider joining the Caravan Club, the Camping and Caravanning Club – or both. These two excellent organisations provide information on everything you need to know about caravanning.

A touring caravan opens up whole new worlds to you. Go away every weekend, take long holidays without worrying about hotel bills. Have a base for sports and hobbies. Discover a whole world of wonderful places.

Each year nearly seventy million holiday nights are spent in caravans. To find out everything you could possibly need to know about it all, give us a ring – we've got a smashing information pack available, absolutely free!

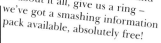

"Frankly, we at Autosleepers think Hannibal would have felt he'd missed out if he'd known about motor caravans. For expeditions large or small, they're ideal.

Auto-Sleepers

AUTOSLEEPERS LTD
Orchard Works
Willersey, nr Broadway
Worcestershire
WR12 7QF
England
Tel: 01386 853338
Fax: 01386 858343

The first huge advantage is that they can be whatever you want them to be. Your own grandstand for the races, a personal beach hut, an idyllic restaurant by the lake or just somewhere to take in the view. It's your personal life support machine, with room to relax, sleep, eat, wash and store your gear. And the second advantage is that they give you real 'get up and go' exploring. It's immediate – you're ready to hit the road whenever you decide to – for a day, a weekend, a holiday (or even crossing the Alps and invading other countries!)

There are two basic styles. The 'coachbuilt' is large and high, custom-built from the chassis up – a dedicated leisure vehicle. The 'high-top' is smaller, ideal for use as an everyday vehicle too, with an elevating roof to give you extra space when you stop. Either will accommodate two, three or four people in style.

And style it is too – one of the pleasures of choosing a motor caravan is discovering just how clever the interiors are. Tables, chairs, cupboards, lockers, wardrobes, beds, kitchens, even toilets and showers – room for everything you think you'll ever need, plus gas and electric appliances too. And perhaps the biggest surprise for the first-timer is the sheer quality and luxury of the fittings.

Autosleeper motor caravans are built onto specially-adapted base vehicles from Ford, Volkswagen, Peugeot, Renault and Mercedes. They are rugged and powerful, driving like cars and handling easily, even if you're a beginner. The cabs are superbly equipped and designed to be driver-friendly. Would-be buyers, as well as choosing their base vehicle, need to decide whether they prefer a petrol engine, a diesel or a turbo-diesel – each has its advantages. Autosleepers has a big choice of models, and all the experience needed to help you work out what's best for you. Pity we couldn't have told Hannibal!"

The **VW** Camper Centre

The VW Camper Centre – by junction 13 of the M25
Bell Weir Garage, Hythe End, Wraysbury, Berks TW19 6HE
Tel: 01784 483438/01753 542260 Fax: 01784 483303

The much-loved – and still very practical – Grand Daddy of all campers! For thousands and thousands of fans the world over, the ONLY way to go exploring. Own a VW and you have style; this is a real fun vehicle, and driving one makes you realise you're part of a club, as fellow owners wave to you as they pass and people stop to admire it nostalgically. And if you want to you can LITERALLY join a club – there are owner's clubs everywhere, rallies, magazines, shows ....!

But is it practical? It most certainly is. Buy one for something between £1,000 and £10,000; there are a million variations on the original 1950's 1131cc model. If you can't find just what you want, one can easily be altered, converted, upgraded or downgraded to suit. You can use it as an everyday vehicle; it's no longer than the average estate car. It's a sound investment too – resale values are always high.

For exploring, it's amazing. Stop, put the brake on and turn it into a home – quicker than a caravan. Use it as it is or raise the elevating roof and sleep four. Add an awning to the side and your living space is more than doubled. Internal fittings incorporate beds, cupboards, tables, seats, cookers, sinks – there are endless permutations. It's easy to drive, mechanically simple, robust and amazingly reliable, with parts easy to find all over Europe and beyond. More than Hannibal could say for his elephants!

Owning your own 'veedub' could be the fun way to low-cost camping for you, whether you want to take the odd weekend on the coast or to go off round the world (there aren't many places VW campers haven't been!). We have a unique deal on all our vehicles from the early 70s to the present day. Buy your vehicle, and off you go; finish your trip and we'll guarantee to buy it back from you – if you can bear to part with it! This can be an amazingly cheap way to take that trip of a lifetime.

Here at the VW Camper Centre we've dealt solely with these wonderful machines for over thirty years – growing up with them is an experience on its own. Come and have a look, and you'll see why!

Three good reasons why a real explorer should choose a tent!

Millets Leisure Limited
Mansard Close, Westgate, Northampton NN5 5DL
Tel: 01604 441111 Fax: 01604 441164

Firstly, tent camping offers you the best of both worlds. You can carry your home on your back and travel wherever you like without any ties, or you can take all the luxuries of home with you and 'live' in the great outdoors with all the luxuries you require. There are tents small enough to carry around with you, and there are others which can accommodate the largest family. We can supply a tent for any purpose, given over 155 stores (which also offer advice and back-up) – more than any other 'outdoor' retailer in the UK.

Tent camping can also be very cheap – we at Millets like to think that camping can give you the freedom to explore the places you want to at a cost that is easily affordable. Quality tents can cost as little as £50. Equally, they can cost as much as £1,000 – it depends on what type of tent you want and what features it has. The important thing is to decide what you need from it. Consider questions such as:

- How many people will the tent sleep?
- Will it offer extra space for rucksack, boots etc?
- Does it need to be small and light enough to carry?
- Is it quick to put up in rainy weather?
- Does it have an inner tent? (Very cheap tents exist which look good value for money but don't have this important feature).

Another vital question – can the shop from which you bought it offer good after-sales service? Modern tents are tough, but they still need looking after – you need to be sure that you'll be able to replace say a flysheet or guyline for the model you've bought. When it comes to accessories, value for money is paramount, and this is where our expertise comes in. Are you going to use that sleeping bag once – in which case you don't need to spend £100 on it – or over and over again, in which case it might be a good investment? And what about cooking and eating equipment, tough yet light enough to carry? We've got it all!

Finally, tent camping is REAL camping – and quite simply, **FUN!**

Barry and Betty Ashworth run 'Camping le Puits' in Normandy. What brought them across the Channel from England and into another world?

"We'd caravanned in France for twenty-five years, so when I took early retirement and the whole family wanted something new to do we decided to set up a site there of our own. My son and daughter had both graduated and were looking for jobs – they were very keen on the project. We decided on Normandy, and found a run-down old farm right on the main Paris-Brittany route and convenient for the ferry ports too. Then we set to work transforming a wilderness into a twenty-five pitch site and a near-derelict house into a home – digging trenches, laying pipes and cables, planting hedges and flower beds for the site and renovating the accommodation.

The local people were wonderful – warm, friendly, helpful and hospitable. We drank so many 'aperitifs' I wonder we got anything done! The workmen were first-rate, particularly Roland the builder-turned-plumber; his family's adopted ours, and vice versa. When we're really busy, they all come down and help out. Anyway, everything did get done, and we're well and truly operational now, with B&B too. The rewards have been tremendous, meeting people from all over the world and making friends. When it's quiet we open up the house and share a drink or two round the log fire with our visitors; we do minibus trips round the 'Cider Route' for them, and then we all sit in the garden and sample our purchases, watching the kids fish roach out of the pond. Believe me, a year in other parts of France has nothing on a year in Normandy. I only wish we could have done this years ago – but, as they say, c'est la vie!"

Régine Jarreton runs 'La Ripole', a little site deep in the Perigord Vert, near the picture-book village of Abjat sur Bandiat. We asked her why!

"'I named the campsite after the little stream which runs through it, 'La Ripole'. I'd returned to the countryside after several years spent studying in big cities. What I discovered was the soundness of the traditional values of simple rural life – and the quality of that life.

I'd inherited a little patch of land from my grandmother, I'd learnt quite a bit about tourism during my studies and most of all I loved working with people – these were the three factors that prompted me to create this site. Last, though, and anything but least (perhaps the most important thing of all), I had my father helping me; he's a master builder, and he helped with all the construction work. Once it was properly equipped, my little patch of land became something which enabled me to get a small loan and develop the business.

Thus I managed to create something from which I get very real pleasure – new contacts and new friends turning up on my doorstep every year. And the campsite means I can live here in the Perigord Vert, where the natural environment is still unspoilt and where a rich cultural and historic heritage counts for something.

For me, it's the visitors and the welcome you give them that's everything. And believe me, when you're thirty-five years old meeting people from different countries really opens your mind and makes life cheerful and interesting. In our village we've got an English pub, run by a really nice English couple who've become totally part of the local scene. We play skittles – and we've got the only French conker team which has ever made it to the World Championships! That's us in the picture, in our regalia!"

The 'Real Exploring' Sites

WE'RE DELIGHTED to present to you a cornucopia of France's loveliest little corners for camping and caravanning – each one in the spirit of 'Real Exploring'. Mostly very small, very quiet and very simple, they are chosen for their position, their intrinsic interest and the absence of intrusive commercialisation.

- USE the centre map to see where the sites are – each one has a number.

- REFER to the pages which follow to find out about their character, their particular features and the area around them

- CHECK in the reference section at the back for details of specific facilities, directions etc.

- PHONE (at a reasonable time) to double-check that the site is open and has space. If a specific facility is important to you (a washing machine, for example, or access to a telephone), check that it's still available. Information given in good faith when this guide was compiled can easily be overtaken by events. If something you need isn't listed, ask the owner's advice.
  By definition, our sites don't provide ultra-lavish facilities – but friendliness, helpfulness and real interest in camping come as standard!

The little flags under the description of the sites tell you which languages the owners speak - not necessarily fluently!

We're committed to real camping, real caravanning and real exploring. Let us know about your adventures, what you think of the sites, what you'd like to see – we'll send a free 'Real Exploring' sticker in exchange for your tales. And if you'd like to nominate a site YOU know for inclusion in next year's guide, we'd love to hear about that too.

1 Real France, not far from Calais. Monsieur Macquet, Verchin.

Not far from Calais is one of the prettiest little bits of France you'll find anywhere – the 'Seven Valleys' at the foot of the Artois hills. Camp here on a lovely little farm site – twelve pitches – and you'll feel yourself to be deep in the heart of France even if you have just popped over for the weekend. Indeed, this is a place made for regular popping over, as well as 'passing through' stops; it's welcoming and well-kept, and at the nearby farm you can can buy bread cooked in a traditional wood-burning oven, tarts as only the French can make them, chickens, rabbits and honey. The little village, Verchin, has a church spire so twisted it's almost a corkscrew; it has a chateau, a park and, we're told, legends. Nearby Hesdin is picture-book pretty, and has one of those Flemish-style churches which when built amiably doubled as market halls. Quite a few English people live here; there's an estate agency called (groaningly) L'Abri Tannique. Five kilometres away is the site of the Battle of Agincourt, or Azincourt, as it is in France. Ponder on the futility of war here, and at nearby Arras and Amiens, each with a sober and dignified northern beauty and traces everywhere of earlier, less happy times; there is something truly sobering about bulletholes in cathedral walls.

☎ 03 21 41 64 87

2 Quiet corner on the Picardy plateau. Monsieur Fontana, La Neuve Rue.

Potter south to Paris on the RN1 for a change; this little site is an ideal place for breaking your journey to or from the Calais ferry. It only has six pitches, and offers you farm camping at its simplest and quietest – a perfect antidote to the horrors of the motorway. It's green and fresh – camping, as you can see, is next to the vegetable patch – and you're very welcome to explore the farm with the friendly Fontana family, who also have a gite here built in the traditional, timber-framed architectural style of this oft-missed region. The farm is in the middle of the village of La Neuve Rue, which is one of those described as 'flowery', and flower-bedecked it certainly is. This is the Picardy plateau, peaceful and open, with tree-lined roads perfect for relaxed touring by car or bike. From here Paris is an hour and a half or so away; if you take the road from nearby Beauvais to Creil you can drive there through the lovely Chantilly forest, and then join the motorway near the airport and the Asterix theme park.

☎ 03 44 46 81 55 •OPEN• ALL YEAR

3 *Camp fires and a cheery welcome on the border with Belgium.*
Madame Alavoine, Brognon.

Light a camp fire here – there's plenty of room, and cheery Madame Alavoine doesn't mind at all. The donkeys, goats and other farm animals don't mind a bit of socialising either – free rides in a little donkey cart for children, and other games too. A happy, relaxed farm site next to a huge forest and with its own little lake in which you can swim.

Here in much-disputed Alsace-Lorraine, you're only seven kilometres from the border with Belgium, so you've a choice of two countries to explore. True Frenchwoman Madame Alavoine only tells us about her own, and points out that there are chateaux, fortified churches, beautiful countryside and much else to see in France. A foray over a border is always fun, though, and Belgium has much to offer (and excellent chips). Whatever else you do here, take yourself off to the Ardennes, straddling the border; breathtakingly scenic, they are a paradise for walkers. The river Meuse runs through, in a deep valley; deer abound, and so do wild boar (which taste delicious; seek out a joint of sanglier and roast it slowly. If you can't find it fresh, try the frozen food department in any reasonably-sized supermarket). Well worth making a town excursion into Charlesville-Mézières, too; it has a spectacular Renaissance square.

☎ 03 24 53 50 27

---

4 *Riverside camping deep in the Ardennes.*
Le Faucon, Nohan-sur-Semoy.

By the edge of the dramatic river Semoy, deep in the dramatic Ardennes. A really friendly little site from which to enjoy this stunning setting, with all manner of activities on offer, notably canoeing (for which this river is ideally suited) fishing and cycling – you can hire bikes on site. Nature rambles, with a guide, are available too, and are possibly the best way to discover this area of dense forests and wonderful pine-laden air; energetically-challenged explorers will feel fitter just by breathing it in. Some interesting-looking restaurants nearby, some offering 'Ardennes specialities', many of which are based on the game with which the forest abounds. For a fascinating excursion from here, cross the border and take the road into Luxembourg, a glorious little country where everyone seems to speak four languages (sometimes in the course of one sentence) and the car park machines take money in one currency and give change in another.

☎ 03 24 41 26 78 Fax 03 24 41 75 58

5 *Disneyland, Paris, cheese and champagne.*
Le Moulin d'en Haut, near Meaux.

Somewhere among our readers will be an equine expert who can tell me the breed of this fine French gentleman – the one with the short fat-hairy legs. I've never seen his like elsewhere. He lives on a farm called 'The High-up Mill', between Paris and the Champagne area. Camp there by the edge of a river in lush countryside, near a village of 600 inhabitants. This is an ideal base for Disneyland, which is only 25km away, close enough to drive in and out each day. Perfect for that other great fantasy too, Paris – you could get the train for the 50km journey from here. The farm's not far from Meaux, a pretty little town famous for its wonderful Brie cheese, triumphantly unpasteurised and absolutely delicious. Beware, if you're (laudably) tempted to buy a whole great cartwheel of it – keep what you're not ready to use immediately in the fridge, or it'll develop a life of its own. A wonderful thing to do is to hire a cabin cruiser and cruise the Marne between Meaux and Paris. Arriving in the centre of Paris by boat is one of those few experiences which really IS unforgettable; discover the charming Canal St Martin, like a 1930's film set, right in the heart of the city. And of course, you're near the Champagne region, which merits a month's exploring.

☎ **01 64 36 61 34**

6 *Farm camping with farm produce a-plenty.*
Ferme de la Croix-Villière, Neuville-Day.

Better be hungry if you camp here – this lovely little farm site (twelve pitches) has a shop selling local produce – *including* milk, wild boar, honey, jam, pheasant pate, duck pate, chicken pate, sweets, snails, cider, apple juice and a range of made-up dishes! And, should you still be peckish, the baker calls every day, breakfast can be supplied at the farmhouse and the village has a restaurant. Work it all off (if you can move) by helping out with the farm animals or a game of ping-pong or boules – if you can't, simply sit and admire the view from the site of a thirteenth-century chateau. This is a happy place to be, with much to do all around; the river Aisne is nearby, plus the Canal des Ardennes with a spectacular flight of locks (some pretty spectacular fish in both); you can visit the chateau or the nearby lake where watersports are on offer, walk or ride in the forest. Or wander along and see what's new in the farm shop today.

☎ **03 24 71 44 19 Fax 03 24 71 68 15** •OPEN• ALL YEAR

Foreign Fields

Real
Exploring in NORTH EAST FRANCE

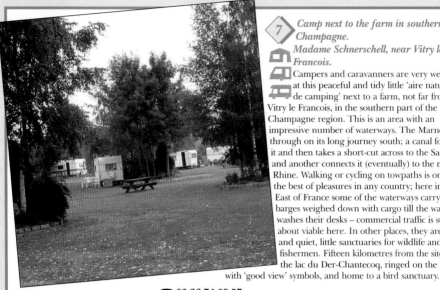

7 *Camp next to the farm in southern Champagne.*
Madame Schnerschell, near Vitry le Francois.

Campers and caravanners are very welcome at this peaceful and tidy little 'aire naturelle de camping' next to a farm, not far from Vitry le Francois, in the southern part of the Champagne region. This is an area with an impressive number of waterways. The Marne flows through on its long journey south; a canal follows it and then takes a short-cut across to the Saone, and another connects it (eventually) to the mighty Rhine. Walking or cycling on towpaths is one of the best of pleasures in any country; here in the East of France some of the waterways carry big barges weighed down with cargo till the water washes their desks – commercial traffic is still just about viable here. In other places, they are tiny and quiet, little sanctuaries for wildlife and fishermen. Fifteen kilometres from the site is the lac du Der-Chantecoq, ringed on the map with 'good view' symbols, and home to a bird sanctuary.

☎ **03 26 74 09 57**

---

8 *Lovely town and lovely lakes.*
Camping Hautoreille Bannes, near Langres.

A lovely international welcome here from Mani, who's from Germany, and Elisabeth, who's Swiss – they're happy to speak English, French or German! Quiet, country camping, surrounded by fields, on the edge of a village which has a restaurant and 6km (cycling distance) from the town of Langres, which claims a place in the Top Fifty of beautiful French towns and is famous for its bracing winters.
Langres is close enough to the border to have been fortified for centuries – at least since the third one – and has four kilometres of ramparts, around which you can walk and from which you can see for miles. It's a town of tiny roads and beautiful buildings; it has a splendid

cathedral and (like most of France) is the birthplace of a famous philosopher. Its other celebrated citizen is a young nurse who in the seventeenth century left home and hearth to evangelize the 'New World'.
Outdoor explorers will enjoy the four glorious lakes near the camp site. There are child-safe beaches, swimming, sailing, surfing, and (writes Elisabeth) the sport-fishing of carpes. Ideal walking and cycling country too.

☎ **03 25 84 83 40**

9 Tiny site, *"one big international family".*
La Renaudine, near Vesoul.

The owners of this farmhouse warmly invite you to camp on one of their six pitches and, if you wish, share their 'table d'hote' with their bed and breakfast guests "as one big international family". Accept their invitation; this little site on the way over to the Jura and Switzerland is a winner. On the edge of the village, surrounded by trees, it has views over neighbouring settlements and the forest; in the distance you can see the Vosges (famous for odd but habit-forming pine pastilles). Rabbits, poultry, pigs, sheep etc for kids to discover – and the farmer will take you into the village by pony-trap, pulled by the gentle and very beautiful Pimpante! All this, plus wonderful food and all the help you need to explore the treasures of this beautiful region. Difficult to imagine wanting to leave the site, but if you do, there's much to see; including several museums, a glass factory and some pretty little towns. Fishing and canoeing just down the road. This is one of those places where you make friends for life.

☎ **03 84 49 82 34**

10 *Poetry and passion in the Jura.*
Renee and Claude Monnin, Charmoille.

'The scent of drying hay, the perfume of the elder-tree and the lime in flower; hot night, cool night, passionate night, stormy night, clear night lit by the moon – that's what it means, a night on a farm'.

Renee and Claude sent us this poem to describe camping on their farm. They were pretty poetic, not to mention passionate, about their region, too – the magnificent Jura, where France meets Switzerland. They live in a beautiful old 'comptoise' farmhouse, and their little campsite is very much part of the life of the farm; as you can see, a variety of small beasties scampers around, and there are donkies and ponies to ride and farm produce to buy. Their region, they explain, has not yet been discovered by big-scale tourism; nature and agriculture live harmoniously together in a landscape famous for its flowers and rare birds. Pure mountain rivers and dramatic canyons abound; there are numerous marked walks to follow and lovely old villages to visit. In the winter, this is ski country; at other times, it is calm, tranquil and, in their view, pure paradise.

☎ **03 81 44 30 29**

Foreign Fields

11 *Farm camping in the undiscovered Pays d'Othe.*
Ferme des Hauts-Frenes.

A super little farm site (six pitches) in one of those secret little pockets of France which are rich in interest and yet (so far at least) retain their innocence in a world where everything that can be labelled 'culture' or 'heritage' is packaged and pasteurised. This is the 'Pays d-Orthe'. Between Troyes, historic city of the Champagne country, and Auxerre, historic city of Burgundy, it shows a certain bloody-mindedness in being famous for its cider. An undulating land of orchards and villages described as 'sauvage et rude' (rugged and unspoilt). Here there is cider in the very air, with museums and presses to visit and plenty of product to taste and buy. Lots of nice forest country to roam near here too.

A lovely town to explore is Auxerre, perched on the river Yonne with a surprisingly large inland harbour – bump into chatty Dutchman Paul who runs his boat hire business here and you'll be there for a while. The farm is pretty, with its old stone buildings, and situated right in the heart of a little village; Monsieur and Madame Lambert are hugely proud of their little corner of France. Possibly one of those places to which one gets addicted! Bike hire and B&B here too.

☎ **03 25 42 15 04 Fax 03 25 42 02 95** •OPEN• ALL YEAR

---

12 *A farm in Old France.*
Au Relax Vert, near St Sauveur-en-Puisay.

Take the N7 south from Paris, and when you get to Briare, where Monsieur Eiffel built his famous canal aqueduct, you'll find yourself following the Loire valley down into western Burgundy. Leave the main road and head for Auxerre; you'll discover a little bit of old France. Deeply wooded countryside, chateaux, unspoilt villages and everywhere that feeling of living a little in the past and being very happy about it. Monsieur and Madame Morin are farmers, keen to welcome you to their pretty little site and to their serendipitous region. The nearby Chateau de St Fargeau has spectacular

staged events and 'son et lumiere' evenings depicting the last thousand years of the area's history. Pottery's been made here for that long at least, and you'll see it for sale everywhere. The past survives well in this time-warp territory; there are prehistoric grottos, churches with medieval wall paintings a-plenty – and, for bric-a-brac hunters, excellent junk shops. Real explorers can go big-game hunting here (with a camera); the superb Boutissaint Natural Park ("a thousand acres of happy forest") is anything but a zoo. Bison, wild boar and all manner of creatures with sharp pointy bits run wild here and, visitors are warned, cannot be considered to be under the control of the management. Back at the Morins' farm the animals definitely are; they're all part of the scene for campers, as are free fishing on the little lakes, pedalos, boules and games for the kids. A place to restore the soul.

☎ **03 86 45 53 83 Fax 03 86 45 59 33**

13 *Farm/auberge in the magical Morvan.*
Les Chatelaines, Avallon.

Camp by this little farm auberge/restaurant and have wonderful French country food and wine on your doorstep. You can be sure you won't eat badly – this is Burgundy, after all. Not the wine-label country further east, with its haute cuisine and rather haute prices, but the old country where absolutely nothing's nouvelle, let alone the cuisine. Regale yourself, as the French say, with boeuf bourguignon, game and local ham, all cooked of course in sauces saturated with most things bad for you; Burgundian snails are the best in the world; you can drink wine from Chablis just up the road and, if you're brave, Marc de Bourgogne, a sort of brandy-cum-tractor-fuel indigenous to the region. And you're in the heart of the Morvan, a spectacular national park merely metres from the A6 motorway and seemingly known only to Parisiens, who flock here at weekends. It's a region of high hills, deep forests and mountain streams; Avallon (where the site is) and Vezelay are the most famous of its beautiful hilltop towns and villages. Locals will tell you about the 'hillbillies' who live in the wildest bits, rarely with electricity and telephones and with wells for water; they have a dialect and a dress of their own. Here you see pre-war 'Maigret' Citroens peeping out of barns. Walks and cycle trails everywhere.

☎ **03 86 34 16 37 Fax 03 86 34 55 95** •OPEN• ALL YEAR

14 *Camping on a Sheep Museum.*
La Reserve, near Decize.

The Ryan family lived in England until Marie-Georges inherited an ancient Burgundian farmhouse which had belonged to, but not housed, her family for centuries. Despite its being in that condition described even by French estate agents as 'lamentable', they fell in love with it, moved themselves across the channel and set about putting it to rights. Theirs is possibly the world's only campsite on a sheep museum. You can have a 'conducted visit' of the rare breeds on site, see traditional wool processing and if you wish sign up for one of Marie-George's wonderful craft courses – ring her for details. This is a cheery, relaxed place – minimal facilities and six pitches – where kids and animals run amok and from which you can discover the departement of the Nievre, so buried in the heart of France that even the French forget it's there. Its Tourist Department describes it as the 'green land of living waters', and that it certainly is; perhaps the loveliest of its waters is the enchanting Canal du Nivernais, built to take the wood from the forests to Paris. Walk or cycle the towpath from nearby Cercy la Tour (which perversely has no tower); look out for kingfishers, red squirrels and at night barn owls. A car ride will take you to ancient Moulins Engilbert, where the white Charollais cattle are traded; try the restaurant in the 'Hotel Bon Laboureur' or, for sophistication, 'Le Cadran'. Or drive into nearby Decize, built on an island in the Loire by the Romans, with a lovely market. A real explorer's paradise.

☎ **03 86 50 04 34 Fax 03 86 50 59 24** •OPEN• ALL YEAR

Foreign Fields

15 *Enchanted valley of the Canal du Nivernais.*

Monsieur Goguelat, La Collancelle.

La Collancelle is a deep cutting through which passes the fairytale Canal du Nivernais on its way to Paris. It is wooded, full of wild flowers and creatures and supremely tranquil, the silence broken only by birdsong and boats. Artists live in the little lock cottages; the photographer who captured this one caught the atmosphere in words, too: *"A different place to be. Time and space spread out further than you can believe. You learn to see, and to hear; the earth seen in the water, and the water seen in silence."* You can cycle the towpath all the way to Paris from here; or go a few miles from village to village, overtaking the barges, helping them at the locks and buying produce from the lock-keepers. Bring a little boat of your own or hire one (ask the Tourist Office); the fishing's good in the canal (lots of fishing competitions are held here; quite a spectacle, involving a great deal of wine and ceremony). There are six pitches on Monsieur Goguelat's farm nearby; he rears the white beef cattle of this undulating region at the foot of the Morvan hills, and has all you need for cheap, cheerful but comfy camping. Nearby Baye has expansive lakes; Nivernais towns such as Chatillon-en-Bazois and Corbigny are infinitely explorable.

☎ **03 86 22 41 89**

16 *In the land of the chateaux of the Loire.*

Ferme de Prunay, near Chateaurenault.

This is the heart of the Loire valley chateau country – five of them within twenty miles of this site (Chenonceaux, Chambord, Chaumont, Amboise and Blois). They're all lovely. Chenonceaux, designed by ladies, is a real fairy-tale confection, Chaumont is severely fortified, Amboise is in the heart of its picture-book pretty town – there's a month's exploring here for lovers of French architecture in the grand style. Nearby Blois has not only a chateau but also an impressive history; in days gone by it was the centre of political (and royal) life in France. Among its famous sons are a clockmaker, a chocolatier and a religious-rebel-cum-pressure-cooker-inventor, whose statue is

worth a photo as well as a detour. This is vineyard country too, of course (try Touraine Mesland, just up the road from the site); pretty countryside with quiet back roads perfect for exploring by bike. To the west is the Sologne, low-lying and mysterious with its lakes and game birds, and to the east Tours, where, it's said, the best French in France is spoken. Camp on Monsieur Fouchault's happy little site in the midst of it all and enjoy walks, fishing, a game of boules or a taste of his farm produce.

☎ **02 54 70 02 01/06 08 42 17 56 Fax 02 54 70 11 53**

17 *Wine-making farm in the Loire valley region.*

La Charmoise, near Contres.

This little farm produces, among other things, Vin de Touraine. See how it's made, and sample the odd gallon. If you'd like to cook yourself something to go with it, Monsieur Foinard will happily supply you with a barbecue and with plenty of vine cuttings to burn on it. There are lovely marked walks on the site (acres of land) and cycle routes too, through forest and pretty, varied countryside. As well as the spectacular famous-name chateaux all around, there are little ones on less-beaten tracks; Troussay, just to the north, has a nice one. And as well as the spectacular famous-name Loire, there are little rivers, too – its own tributary, confusingly called the Loir, and the Cher. From which this whole Département, Loir and Cher, gets its name. All of it's worth exploring; it has vineyards, dramatic caves and troglodyte houses carved out of cliffs, wonderful wall paintings in its churches, Roman remains, beautiful buildings and some of the best formal gardens in Europe.

☎ **02 54 79 55 15**

18 *Farm camping by an ancient pilgrim route.*

La Belle Etoile, near Vendôme.

Six pitches on Monsieur and Madame Ablancourt's farm in the rich-in-history bit of the Loir (not Loire) valley west of Vendôme. The great mediaeval pilgrimage route to Santiago de Compostela in Spain led through this area, and little churches, hospitals and lodgings where monks and the Knights Templar sheltered and cared for the travellers. Earlier lodgings too – troglodyte caves built into the relatively soft cliffs, some of them still used today. Vendôme, as well as providing explorers with provisions of every kind, is an exceptionally pretty place, and the road from there to the site is one of those marked with a green line on Michelin maps, meaning particularly scenic. All in all a fascinating little corner of France. The site has its own little lake where you can fish, and there's pony-trekking, hunting, golf , tennis and a free swimming pool nearby. Farm produce is available, and meals can be cooked for you by arrangement.

☎ **02 54 72 00 89** •OPEN• ALL YEAR

19 In the centre of France near Sancerre. La Huchette, Argent sur Saudre.

Camp under trees in blossom at Jacqueline and Jack Huet's pretty little site with a stream, a lake, lots of trees and flowers and forest all around. This is an excellent stop-on-the-way south-from-Paris site, whether you're travelling on the A71/E11 motorway or on the infinitely more interesting (but somewhat lorry-ridden) N7 following the Loire. It's on the very edge of the great forest that further west becomes the Sologne, an odd area which manages to be both wooded and marshy at the same time. Go east and you meet the series of nice old towns which span the Loire – Gien, Briare (which spans it in some style, thanks to Monsieur Eiffel of tower fame), Cosne sur Loire and then famous but remarkably unperturbed Sancerre. There, and at nearby (equally famous) Pouilly, there are *caves* to visit and wine to taste and buy; don't ask the locals which ones are best unless you have a week to spare. Just up the road, tiny Chavignol is famous all over France for its goats' droppings – crottins, little round cheeses that taste better than they might, given their name. If you're travelling on the motorway, look out for the rest area with a big sign announcing that it marks the very centre of France.

☎ **02 48 73 32 61**

20 Country cuisine, wine and monks in Burgundy. Ferme-Auberge St Malo, near Tournus.

Friendly auberge camping on a farm in the south of Burgundy, close to the A6 motorway. In lovely buildings in a pretty and restored hamlet bedecked with flowers, this little country restaurant serves traditional 'peasant' cuisine (it's all relative, though, in Burgundy) and local wine, local being Macon, or at a pinch Beaujolais. Twenty-five pitches for campers, lots of room and lots of shade and a river with a bathing pool running through. Wine, farm produce and crafts on sale. Venture out from here and you'll find Wine Routes in every direction; nearby Tournus is an ancient and attractive town, particulary when viewed from the bridge across the Saone. Cluny, site of an ancient abbey and one of the best-known tourist sites in France, is a scenic drive from the farm. In 1098 the Pope declared that the abbey, by then a major intellectual and spiritual centre, was 'the light of the world'; alas, the monks grew rich, powerful and degenerate, causing St Bernard to grumble that the bishops "couldn't move four steps from their houses without sixty or more horses in their train – couldn't the light of the world shine just as brighly in a silver candelabra as a gold one?". That was the beginning of the end; it remains though a spectacular and atmospheric place. More modern ecclesiastical influences of interesting vitality can be found just to the north, at Taizé.

☎ **03 85 92 21 47/03 85 92 20 63 Fax 03 85 92 22 13**

21. A walled orchard haven just off the main road.

Chez Gros Jean, St Sulpice les Feuilles.

A handful of pitches here in this walled orchard with its own well. This little farm in the Haute Vienne is only five kilometres from the motorway, yet feels as if it's deep in some other world. It belongs to Ann and David Scott – they love to have visitors, and feel they've got the perfect location for them (with more land outside the orchard too should you wish to be alone!). There are lakes all around (two just up the road) and forests, and the nice little town of St Sulpice les Feuilles is an easy walk or bike ride away. Take the main road south and you have an easy drive into Limoges, famous the world over for its fine porcelain and enamel ware; the town still supplies vast quantities of porcelain to the tables of France. There are museums to visit and factory bargains to be had here. A region for quiet wandering or cycling on peaceful roads. And one besotted with chestnuts; at one time they were the staple diet here, and they're still eaten in every imaginable (and unimaginable) form.

☎ **05 55 76 67 89 (phone and fax)** •OPEN• ALL YEAR

22. Fine views from a house on a hill.

'Les Quatre Vents', Bessines sur Gartempe.

The Pickerings, originally from England, own this lovely little corner; their house sits in splendid isolation on top of a hill, and whichever way you look there are breathtaking views – artistic and photographic explorers will be in their element. They can take up to six tents, caravans or motorhomes; there's a cool pine glade and an orchard, and for those hot sunny days a swimming pool. It's set in the deep valley of the Gartempe river, which is crossed by two Gothic bridges, and borders on to both the rural area of the Basse Marche country and the wooded, mountainous region of the Ambazac. Take a bike ride or a stroll into Bessines (four kilometres) and you'll find cobbled streets, a lovely old church and flowers everywhere. Speciality food shops sell those intriguing local delicacies that just demand to be tried out, and there are restaurants and bars and a market on Sundays. A twenty-minute walk from the site following a peaceful woodland path takes you to Lake Sagnet, where there's every imaginable sort of sport in and on the water and quite a few round it. B&B available too.

☎ **05 55 76 37 26** •OPEN• ALL YEAR

Foreign Fields

23 *In the steps of Richard the Lionheart.*
Les Vigeres, near Chalus.

Richard the Lionheart met his end just ten kilometres from this little site, but that didn't deter his fellow-countrymen Robert and Shirley. They live right on the Richard the Lionheart Trail, just down the road from the village of Le Chalard. Occupied by the English army during the Hundred Years' War, and where the building that was their headquarters is still called the 'Maison des Anglais' (things move slowly in the Limousin!). Here too is an eleventh-century fortified church and a monastery that played an important role in the Third Crusade to Jerusalem. It's one of those areas where you'll find things you never dreamt were here – including a gold mine still actively exploited, and particles of the precious stuff in all the local streams and rivers. The site is supremely tranquil, with magnificent views, walks through woodlands and a wonderful 'natural spring' lake for swimming, with a sandy beach and swinging rope. Robert and Shirley have been here for five years now; their clientele keeps coming back and, they say, are more friends than customers.

☎ 05 55 09 37 22 Fax 05 55 09 93 39

24 *Simple farm camping in a land of legends.*
Ferme du Petit-Chaumeix, near Boussac.

The Creuse region is another of those that time has passed by. Monsieur Ladet's farm near the little town of Boussac is a place to camp and discover the simplicity of a way of life that hasn't changed a great deal in a long while. "You can stay here in perfect tranquility and simply enjoy nature" he says. There's a river for fishing nearby; he has a boules pitch, produce for sale and an exhibition of agricultural implements by way of excitement, and a big communal room for campers. His village, he says, is tiny. Nearby Boussac is a fortified town with a formidable chateau, a goodly sprinkling of restaurants and most things necessary for the provisioning of expeditions. Some odd things lie nearby. At Toulx Sainte Croix is an inexplicable jumble of enormous stones; these strange rocks on their wild hillside create an atmosphere that sends shivers down the spine. Local legend has it that buried under them is the treasure of the ancient town of Toul. Every now and then (we're told) a golden calf springs out from its hiding place here, breathing fire. Sinners are in trouble at this point; if, however, it's someone with a clear conscience that the calf meets, it'll lead him to the treasure, which he must distribute to all, thereby bringing in an age of wealth and happiness.

☎ 05 55 65 06 46

25 *In the grounds of an ancient abbey.*
Abbaye de Prébenoît, near Guéret.

It took thousands of people, most of them volunteers, more than twenty-five years to restore this ancient Cisterican abbey; they came from all over the world, bringing with them materials, skills and moral support for this enormous project. The 'before and after' pictures are fascinating. Now this lovely building's been saved, and is making a real contribution to the local economy. It's a place for the local community to use and for holidaymakers to stay – there's accommodation for fifty people inside. In its five acres of parkland, bordered by a stream and equipped with picnic tables and children's play equipment, you can camp – truly a site with a difference. "A secret for everyone" is the slogan of the Creuse Tourist Department; it's a secret well worth discovering. If you do nothing else in this hidden region at least explore Aubusson to the south, famous for centuries for its tapestries. The town is pretty and full of history; you can visit the tapestry museum and see this wonderful craft being practised. Nearby is the spectacular man-made Lac de Vassiviére.

☎ **05 55 80 78 91/05 55 83 80 95 Fax 05 55 67 74 28**

26 *Glorious scenery on the edge of the Massif.*
La Loge, near St. Etienne.
"I'm sending you a photo" said Monsieur Granjon *"of our magnificent countryside, which is not short of charm, and which I hope lots of your readers will have the pleasure of discovering".* ANY of our readers travelling on the A6/A7 motorway, or one one of the various main roads passing through St. Etienne, should seriously consider making the very short detour necessary to do just that. This is the heart of the Pilat Regional Park, on the edge of the Massif Central, which isn't Central but is certainly Massif (it covers about a sixth of France). Explorers who pore over maps will find plenty of squiggly roads edged with green (means they're very scenic), high points marked in metres running to four figures and 'view' symbols

everywhere. Monsieur Granjon's site, on his farm, has twenty pitches and, he says, is ideal for reposing. If, that is, you can drag yourself away from this scenery; there are walks and bike trails in abundance and wherever you look there are views like this. Chateaux and museums hidden away for you to visit; you could plunge deep into the Auvergne from here, land of volcanoes.

☎ **04 77 39 65 25**

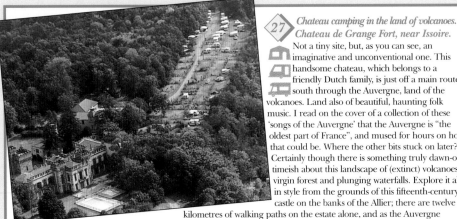

27 *Chateau camping in the land of volcanoes.*
Chateau de Grange Fort, near Issoire.

Not a tiny site, but, as you can see, an imaginative and unconventional one. This handsome chateau, which belongs to a friendly Dutch family, is just off a main route south through the Auvergne, land of the volcanoes. Land also of beautiful, haunting folk music. I read on the cover of a collection of these 'songs of the Auvergne' that the Auvergne is "the oldest part of France", and mused for hours on how that could be. Where the other bits stuck on later? Certainly though there is something truly dawn-of-timeish about this landscape of (extinct) volcanoes, virgin forest and plunging waterfalls. Explore it all in style from the grounds of this fifteenth-century castle on the banks of the Allier; there are twelve kilometres of walking paths on the estate alone, and as the Auvergne covers 1,500,000 acres you're unlikely to run out of routes. Routes are important here; the ones to the many castles have tales of the past to tell. There's a 'craft route' and, given the spectacular flora of this region, a Daffodil Way, an Iris Way and a Gentian Way. You can take the route too to the top of Mont Dome (the highest peak); the first 1,440 metres you can do by car, the remaining twenty-four you must do on foot. Get there and you'll find the Romans got there first, and built a temple to Mercury, messenger of the gods. The chateau is splendid, visitable and functions as the centre of the site; you can swim, fish, raft, ride and even take a six-day canoe trip on the river.

☎ 04 73 71 05 93/04 73 71 02 43 Fax 04 73 71 07 69 •OPEN• ALL YEAR

28 *Friendly farm camping in mysterious country.*
Monsieur Louradour, near Ussel.

One for SERIOUS explorers. This little farm site on the border between Corrèze and Cantal is surrounded on the map by all sorts of fascinating and mysterious things. You'll see, for example, that (believe it or not) it's in the valley of the Dordogne, which starts up in the Auvergne; you'll see that there's a barrage nearby and gorges everywhere with the little blue 'view' signs. One wonders, though, about the 'route des Ajustants' and the 'Pont des Ajustants', just to the south west – what were they ajusting? And why on the map to the east of the barrage does it say 'uranium'? What are the 'orgues' shown near Bort-les-Orgues? To cap it all, the road map shows an airport sign here. Looking at the picture, a goodly sprinkling of explorers make their way here, and with this countryside it's not difficult to understand why. English readers who, having travelled this far south are now suffering cheddar cheese withdrawal symptoms will be relieved to know that the Cantal region produces a hard cheese closer to the beloved substance than anything else in France. An acceptable substitute in an emergency.

☎ 05 55 94 50 52

29 *Walking shops and wild fruits in the Cantal.*
Monsieur Mouillier, near St Flour.

This is a cheery and well-organised little site where 'walking shops' visit to make sure you have all you need for the all-important business of eating. Monsieur Mouillier also tells us that from here you can go out collecting wild fruits and hunting mushrooms. Another one of those places not much further from the motorway than the service area, but with infinitely more charm – stop here if you're on the motorway route over the Massif from Clermont Ferrand. This is the Cantal (cheesophiles see previous page), near the town of St Flour, which sits high on an outcrop of volcanic rock. A railway viaduct built by Monsieur Eiffel is yet more proof that he built more than towers. There are pretty spectacular lakes and reservoirs close by, and a lovely scenic drive south from Ruynes-en-Margeride which follows the valley of the river Truyère and brings you back onto the motorway a little further south. The site's in the Margeride mountains, which are extensive, lofty and made for pottering through.

☎ 04 71 23 40 68

30 *A warm welcome and wonderful farm cooking.*
Camping de l'Etang, Champs-sur-Tarentaine.

"Our little bit of the Cantal region is one where the old traditions have a firm hold" says Madame Gérard. *"Our farm's on a plateau, looking over the Puy de Sancy. The welcome is simple but warm – our visitors know we're pleased to see them. The meals we serve in our little restaurant are typical of our 'deep Auvergne', and very sociable"*. This is a happy place, a simple farm site with lots of space on the edge of a little lake where you can fish; the cows get mixed up with the campers sometimes, but it doesn't seem to matter. The 'restaurant' conjures up regional specialities based on the produce of the farm – you can buy dishes to take away, and Madame Gérard has

home-made jam and honey for sale too. If you're ever going to learn to play petanque, this is the place to do it; if you're going to learn to wind-surf or canoe (or just walk, fish, cycle or enjoy the view) you'll find this magnificent lake just four kilometres away. The little town of Champs-sur-Tarentaine, surrounded by forests, waterfalls and scenery like this, has shops, bars, restaurants and a market on Thursdays; within minutes of it are a mining museum, a butterfly museum and a radio museum.

☎ 04 71 78 71 36

Foreign Fields

31 ▷ Getting to know ways of life.
La Baraque, Espalem.

Among the 'proposed activities' listed by Monsieur and Madame Delair who own this little site is 'getting to know ways of life'. They could have written our introduction. You don't have to go far off the beaten motorway to meet people who have another way of life and are happy to share it with you for a while. The Delairs tell us too that they speak French, a little English and the local dialect. The sign on their gate bids you welcome in four languages – 'La Baraque', by the way, means a hut, not a military-style barracks (although no doubt one word led to the other). This campsite is anything but military; it's a working farm (beef and dairy cattle, sheep, cereals) with six pitches; produce on site, boulangerie three kilometres away. As well as getting to know ways of life, you can explore the dramatic river valley with its 'geology trails', walk, go trout fishing, visit chateaux from various periods, see works of art, discover Blesle, one of France's most beautiful villages, find numerous ancient churches and climb a whole collection of mountains.

☎ 04 71 76 20 50

32 ▷ Evenings (and discussions) round the camp fire.
Les Marodons, near Thiers.

"Evenings round the camp fire and discussions" are what Monsieur and Madame Halper like. They speak French and English, and run their friendly little ten-pitch site at Noalhat, which is not far from the motorway going west from Clermont Ferrand, home of Michelin tyres. It's a grassy meadow on their farm, shaded by surrounding trees; farm produce is available, as is fishing, and it's a stopping-off place for horseriders. They also enjoy petanque competitions – and everything that involves meeting their visitors. Just down the road there's a beach on the river where you can swim; come in the winter and you can ski near here too. The nearest town is Thiers, which George Sand called 'the black town' – we've shown you a picture of it so that you can see that it isn't; it's a sort of red and gold and terracotta town, with old buildings tumbling down the hillside. Thiers is famous for its cutlery; you can visit an impressive museum and a cutlery workshop. There are some good modern buildings here of that unmistakeably French style, a contemporary art centre and some matter-of-opinion type statues sitting on a hillside.

☎ 04 73 94 10 30

33 Site by the sea on the Normandy coast.
Monsieur Massu, Pirou, Cotentin Peninsular.

Monsieur Massu's farm is right on the coast between Cherbourg and Mont St Michel, and from one of the restaurants in the village you can see across to Jersey. The fine, sandy beach is six kilometres long, and the tide goes out for miles, uncovering innumerable rock pools where you can harvest shellfish and bring them back to eat on the site. Wash them down perhaps with some of the farm cider Monsieur Massu sells; he has eggs, milk and other produce too. Camp here and be greeted with a warm welcome and plenty of tourist information – there's a lot to discover here. Pirou is a nice little place which has a market three times a week and is home to the oldest chateau in Normandy (guided tours every day); nearby there's an immense pine forest, wonderful for walking and cycling – explorers may find the ruins of an old mill. Easy from here to join the hordes of tourists at Mont St Michel, or to cut across the peninsular to visit the D-Day landing beaches; when you've done all that, Monsieur Massu will be delighted to see you back at the site, which is, he reminds us, a long way from pollution and from noise. One of those 'handy for the ferry' places which you won't want to leave.

☎ **02 33 45 29 29 Fax 02 33 45 88 26**

34 *Warmest of welcomes in the very heart of Normandy.*
Camping Le Puits, St Martin des Besaces.

You'll have met Mr Ashworth and his family on page fourteen. They'd love to see you at their happy little site right in the heart of Normandy – easy to get to from Cherbourg and also on the main Paris-Brittany route. This is Calvados and cider country par excellence; real explorers might like to get to the bottom of the *trou Normand*. The landscape is rolling and pretty, and in the lush green fields the cattle whose milk makes the famous cheeses and cream wander – look for real Normandy Camembert, made with unpasteurised milk, and leave it to ripen for a few days; eat JUST before it goes critical. Camp in the shade of the apple trees; the site has everything you need. Bayeux with its famous tapestry; the D-Day

beaches, Mont St Michel, historic Domfront in the Regional Park, Little Switzerland, rivers for canoeing and fishing and the lovely Cotentin coast with its lively and picturesque fishing villages are all within easy reach. There are lovely walking, cycling and equestrian trails from the site. Wander into the village and you'll find a museum telling you about the lovely 'bocage' country, and nearby, would you believe, bungee jumping!

☎ **02 31 67 80 02 (phone and fax)**

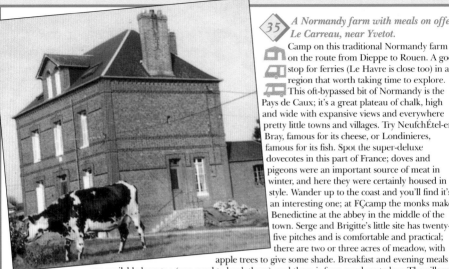

35 ▷ A Normandy farm with meals on offer. Le Carreau, near Yvetot.

Camp on this traditional Normandy farm on the route from Dieppe to Rouen. A good stop for ferries (Le Havre is close too) in a region that worth taking time to explore. This oft-bypassed bit of Normandy is the Pays de Caux; it's a great plateau of chalk, high and wide with expansive views and everywhere pretty little towns and villages. Try NeufchÉtel-en-Bray, famous for its cheese, or Londinieres, famous for its fish. Spot the super-deluxe dovecotes in this part of France; doves and pigeons were an important source of meat in winter, and here they were certainly housed in style. Wander up to the coast and you'll find it's an interesting one; at FÇcamp the monks make Benedictine at the abbey in the middle of the town. Serge and Brigitte's little site has twenty-five pitches and is comfortable and practical; there are two or three acres of meadow, with apple trees to give some shade. Breakfast and evening meals are available here too (you need to book them), and there is farm produce to buy. The village is a walk or a cycle ride away, and has shops and a railway station.

☎ 02 35 96 85 57

36 An enchanting corner between Dieppe and the Seine.
Madame Goutchot, Saint-Saëns.

A lovely little corner close to Dieppe and near the motorway to Rouen. Only eight pitches on this farm site on the edge of a forest – a good place for letting off steam and relaxing before or after a long journey. Take your bike and cycle for miles here, through the forest or perhaps on the back road to Neufchatel to try the cheese; this is an area of scenic roads (there are nicer ones between here and Rouen than the motorway) and good views. Dieppe is a place to linger a little; it's a lively and attractive town, still a busy port where you can buy fresh fish and shellfish and eat marvellous 'fruits de mer' meals in the dozens of little restaurants; if you're here on a Saturday, try the market. Or strike south to Rouen, very grand and very busy, for a spot of city exploring and some very good shopping. The Seine takes a windy path from here to Paris; it's fun to abandon the main roads and follow it through picturesque water meadows and pretty villages, crossing the river from time to time, often by ferry. A welcoming little site, where friendly Madame Goutchot loves to see visitors and practise her (very little!) English.

☎ 02 35 34 51 26 (phone & fax) •OPEN• ALL YEAR

37 Orchard camping on a Normandy farm.
Madame Marais, near Cormeilles.

Under the apple trees in this Normandy orchard you can camp and enjoy the exceptionally pretty little patch of countryside around Cormeilles. There are twenty-five pitches here; notice the chickens in front of the little tent in the picture, coming to visit the guests and remind them that this is a farm and they live here too! A lovely eight-kilometre waymarked circular walk from here takes you through valleys, across streams and past farm and manor buildings; Corneilles has lots of the lovely old beamed houses for which Normandy is famous, and plenty of its equally-appreciated cider too. A more adventurous twenty-kilometre walk takes you through the hill country just to the South. Arrange to be at Asnières at midnight on Christmas Eve and you'll see the ancient Druid stone there breathe forth fire and snakes. Explorers who feel that braving the chickens is adventure enough could alternatively wander around the farm and buy fresh produce. A lovely little pocket of Normandy, and a lovely little site from which to enjoy it.

☎ 02 32 42 29 69

38 Seine, sea and lots to see.
Madame Guilliet, near Pont-Audemer.

Madame Guilliet has made a list of all the things there are to see and do near here which she gives to all her campers; there are lots and lots of them, and she doesn't want you to miss any. Her little site is close to the spot where the motorway from Le Havre meets the Paris/Brittany one; you could use it for an overnight stop, but it'd be a shame to miss so much. Close to the site are lovely walks along the Seine and the forest bordering it; you can have a guided trip too to the nearby Vernier marshes. Honfleur, a bustling fishing port with picture-postcard looks, is close; so is Deauville, fashionable and atmospherically-faded seaside resort. There are some very odd things to be found if you wander around a little – there's a Museum of Theatrical Props, and a 'House of Broken Crockery', and if you have ninety minutes to spare at Saint-Pierre-de-Bailleul you can learn all there is to know about the breeding of myocastors. Find time if you can to visit one of the river transport museums on the Seine, and for a real treat take a cruise on this lovely river from Vernon, Poses or Les Andelys. One of the trip boats is called the 'William the Conqueror', a gentleman rather more popular on this side of the Channel than on the other. A very friendly and welcoming little site; lots of space, swings etc for small explorers to let off steam.

☎ 02 32 42 14 52

Foreign Fields

39 *In the spectacular Suisse Normande. Monsieur Monsallier, St Croix sur Orne.*

A site in the Suisse Normande, a part of Normandy with a character all it's own. *'Grandiose panoramas'* says the tourist leaflet; it goes on to describe *"graceful streams wending their way through narrow winding valleys, each turn revealing another delightful view to the eye ... deep, rocky gorges resplendent with broom and heather ... woods and dappled meadows by sparkling waters flowing fresh and cool ... all this and, for the young and the active, delightful walks, the pleasures of boating, fishing, swimming and camping"*. Says it all, really – that's JUST what it's like. It's a lovely area, and this tranquil little twelve-pitch site's perfect for exploring it. On the edge of a forest with the river Orne two hundred metres away, it has spectacular views over the most scenic bit of the St Aubert gorges and is close to a lake and a barrage. You can fish, ride and walk – there's a waymarked path nearby. Or take to exploring by car and discover some real beauty spots. Find your way to the Roche d'Oêtre if you can, and the bridge at Culey le Patry; Flers-de-l'Orne has a moated chateau and there's a chateau-museum at Condé sur Noireau. Falaise is a nice town to explore, featuring, among other things, William the Conqueror's castle.

☎ **02 33 35 05 98 Fax 02 33 36 67 45**

40 *Secret country of the Mayenne. Monsieur Naveau, near Evron.*

A lovely spot in the Mayenne, just north of the Le Mans-Laval road. Six pitches on Monsieur Naveau's farm in the nice little village of Mezangers, first heard about in the sixth century. Arguably not much heard about since, but wander round and you'll find a spectacular chateau by a lake with a magnificent Rennaisance facade, some ancient buildings and an even more ancient church; there's a walking trail to follow. This area is called the 'Coëvrons' – little known, and well worth exploring, with its attention-grabbing mixture of get-out-and-walk-in-it scenery and amazing architecture; there's everything in this little patch from Roman baths to the space-age Tourist Office in Evron. Excellent country for gastronomic explorers too – regional treats spotted recently on menus included fillet of zander with apple slices, roast beef 'fermier du Maine' in Chinon wine, crispy apples in Calvados, pike paté and cream of frogs' legs soup. Lots of interesting farm produce too – try 'pommeau', a traditional and somewhat thermonuclear aperitif made, like so much else round here, from apples. Our little farm site has produce (unspecified) for sale, and meals nearby – it's a friendly place in a most intriguing region.

☎ **02 43 90 65 12**

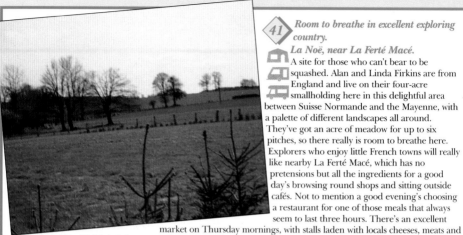

41 Room to breathe in excellent exploring country.
La Noë, near La Ferté Macé.

A site for those who can't bear to be squashed. Alan and Linda Firkins are from England and live on their four-acre smallholding here in this delightful area between Suisse Normande and the Mayenne, with a palette of different landscapes all around. They've got an acre of meadow for up to six pitches, so there really is room to breathe here. Explorers who enjoy little French towns will really like nearby La Ferté Macé, which has no pretensions but all the ingredients for a good day's browsing round shops and sitting outside cafés. Not to mention a good evening's choosing a restaurant for one of those meals that always seem to last three hours. There's an excellent market on Thursday mornings, with stalls laden with locals cheeses, meats and vegetables. All this indulgence can be worked off at the town's leisure lake, sixty-odd acres of swimming, canoeing, sailing, windsurfing and pedalo pedalling. There's also Bagnoles, a spa town with a casino and a golf course, Carrougues which has a fourteenth-century chateau, Falaise and Domfront. For those with ferries in mind, this friendly little site is only an hour and a half from Caen.

☎ **02 33 37 27 71** •OPEN• ALL YEAR

42 A farm welcome off the beaten (race) track.
Monsieur and Madame Boussard, Mansigne, near Le Mans.

Monsieur and Madame Boussard have retired from farming, and now they thoroughly enjoy running their tiny little campsite – especially when the customers turn into friends and keep coming back. They live by the Loir river (a tributary of the big one with the 'e'), to the south of Le Mans. Whizz round the ring road at racing-car speed if you must, then recover from it all in this quiet corner. They have an enormous lake just a short stroll from the site, with little boats for you to mess about it, swimming, fishing golf and lovely walks; the river and the forest compete for your attention.

The local village has two restaurants and a crêperie – Britanny, crêpe capital of the world, is just across the border from here. Not far down the road is the little town of Le Lude, which has a spectacular chateau with guided tours, *son et lumière* displays and sundry spectacles – absolutely not to be missed, says Madame Boussard. There's a porcelain emporium nearby too; Le Mans itself has an 'old town' well worth exploring. Some nice drives and views, especially around Chateau du Loir. Lots of places called 'Chateau' round here – the little Loir is determined not to be outdone by its grand neighbour.

☎ **02 43 46 10 81**

Foreign Fields

Real

Exploring in **WESTERN FRANCE**

43 Lots of fun on a Brittany farm.
Monsieur Cotty, Plouigneau.

"All the entertainment's free" says Monsieur Cotty *"tractor rides, slide shows, our little mini-farm museum, our old farmhouse – and you can wander round the farm as much as you like. There are rabbits, donkeys, piglets, dairy cows, poultry – come and help us look after them all!".* Monsieur Cotty's farm's no distance from the motorway running across the north of Brittany, and no distance either from the ferry port at Roscoff. He has twenty-five pitches, and sent us lots of pictures of explorers (large and very small) up to their eyes in farm animals and smiles. Here the sea is close by – try the lovely drive from nearby Morlaix out along the coast road to Carantec, and then if the tide allows go out to the Isle of Callot – this road is described on the map as 'submersible'. Alternatively, take the road out to the Perros-Guirec peninsular with its spectacular coast, or wander inland a little on scenic roads. No shortages of places to go and things to do in Brittany – this happy farm is a super base.

☎ 02 98 79 11 50

44 A meadow by a chapel in perfect walking and cycling country.
Saint Clair, near Loqueffret.

A brand new site exclusively for explorers under canvas. Six pitches in a meadow – your hosts are Mary and David Archer from England, and they're busy building brand new washing and toilet facilities ready for their opening in April. This lovely little restored chapel is about six hundred years old, and is close to the site in the little hamlet of St Clair where they live, right in the heart of the picturesque western peninsular. From the meadow there's a splendid view south across a wooded valley towards the Black Mountains. Cyclists and walkers will love it here; even in the busy summer season the roads are surprisingly empty, and you can travel for miles across this wide-open countryside, enjoying the tranquility. Find your way to the colourful local markets held in the villages all through the year for a real taste of Breton country life away from the seaside crowds, or maybe take yourself off to Heulgoat, in the centre of the Regional Park, where the lake, wooded valley and huge boulders make a spectacular setting for a picnic. This is hidden Brittany – perfect exploring country – close to Roscoff and well-placed for continuing south.

☎ 02 98 73 94 45 **(phone and fax)** •OPEN• ALL YEAR

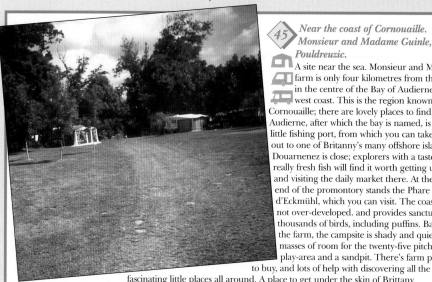

45 *Near the coast of Cornouaille.*
Monsieur and Madame Guinle,
Pouldreuzic.

A site near the sea. Monsieur and Madame's farm is only four kilometres from the beach, in the centre of the Bay of Audierne on the west coast. This is the region known as Cornouaille; there are lovely places to find here. Audierne, after which the bay is named, is a pretty little fishing port, from which you can take a ferry out to one of Britanny's many offshore islands. Douarnenez is close; explorers with a taste for really fresh fish will find it worth getting up early and visiting the daily market there. At the other end of the promontory stands the Phare d'Eckmühl, which you can visit. The coast here is not over-developed. and provides sanctuary for thousands of birds, including puffins. Back on the farm, the campsite is shady and quiet, with masses of room for the twenty-five pitches, a big play-area and a sandpit. There's farm produce to buy, and lots of help with discovering all the fascinating little places all around. A place to get under the skin of Brittany.

☎ **02 98 54 41 14**

46 *Serene country camping in a corner loved by artists.*
Les Genets d'Or, near Bannalec.

Alan and Judy Thomas live here in the summer, and the moment they can organise it will live here all the time. Old customers can't keep away either; it's that sort of place, a lovely countryside setting, perfect for enjoying all that's good about the tourist-trap places, while being just far enough into the country to avoid all that isn't. Their little site is a one-kilometre level walk or ride from the nice little town of Bannalec, which has two rivers and lots of fishing and golf, and where all necessary provisions for expeditions can be found. All around the site are trees – lots of apple and oak. There's a laurel hedge, too, about five feet high – when the Thomas's first came here, it was thirty

feet. They cut it all back by hand, an experience which has left its mark! Close by is the town of Pont-Aven; in days gone by there were lots of mills here driven by the river Aven (which is particularly picturesque here). An old saying talks of "Pont-Aven, a famous town – fourteen mills, fifteen houses". Painters loved it here, particularly Gaugin; you can walk in the 'Bois d'Amour' and follow a trail of posts marking spots which inspired the great artists of the school he founded.

☎ **02 98 39 54 35**

Real

Exploring in **WESTERN FRANCE**

47 *Stud Farm deep in the heart of Brittany.*
Feuntenigou, near Rostrenen.

Camp here – deep in the heart of Brittany – and you'll find yourself on a stud farm which breeds Welsh Cobs ponies! Maybe not as odd as it sounds – the Bretons and the Celts of Wales have much in common (although the horses are not doing too well with picking up the local language). What else will you discover when you explore this beautifully unspoilt area? There was no stopping English owners David and Sybil on this subject. There are villages bright with flowers, ancient churches, lovely manor houses, bustling markets, village fetes and Breton music and dancing. Wander from the site into Rostrenen – not far - and you'll find a little town to explore, with excellent shops and restaurants serving cuisine from 'basic local' to haute. You'll find the Nantes-Brest canal, too – a stroll along its towpath is a pleasure not to be missed. This little site is tranquil and picturesque – no dogs, alas, because of the horses, and the essential electric fences mean it's not ideal for young children. It's perfect though for walking, cycling, riding and fishing – all sorts of water spots too on the nearby lakes. Just minutes from the main road, there are six pitches and acres of space. An interesting and enchanting place, where the deep magic of the Breton heartland will cast its spell.

☎ **02 96 29 12 34 (phone and fax)** •OPEN• ALL YEAR

48 *The simple life in a lovely place.*
Coat Boloï, Pleudaniel.

Eight pitches in a lovely woodland setting just a mile from this glorious chateau. The Staddon family have been here for twenty-five years; they teach English to French youngsters, and lead a simple life growing their own organic vegetables and keeping a few animals. They have some hostel-type accommodation available as well as camping, and provide an ideal setting for school parties and fieldwork trips, given their wonderful environment. They're up in the Trégor region, between L'Armor, in Breton 'the land of the sea' and L'Argoat, 'the land of the woods'. There are footpaths through the woods, and lots of friendly towns to visit by car or bike; the estuary of the river Trieux is a kilometre away, and the Staddons have one or two canoes for hire. Nearby Tréguier has a harbour, a cathedral which is one of the finest in Brittany and a weaving workshop. Paimpol, from where ships once set sail to fish in Icelandic waters, is now a coastal-fishing port and lively resort, where oysters are produced – an ideal place to try the famous 'fruits de mer', or 'platter of the fruits of the sea'. It takes time and a certain dexterity with the impressive array of hardware provided to eat the generally armour-plated 'fruits', but it's very much worth the effort. The Staddons can provide French tuition for English speakers, and can help too with information and advice on living in France – administration, education, health care and much more.

☎ **02 96 20 16 59** •OPEN• ALL YEAR

40

49 *In the grounds of a manor house.*
Manoir de la Villeneuve, near
Lamballe.

Camp in the grounds of the handsome Manoir de la Villeneuve, a fine Brittany stone building. From here it's a short walk or cycle ride into Lamballe, a sizeable market town which has had a stormy history. In 1591, it was beseiged by the famous Captain La Noüe, who with an iron hook instead of an arm was perhaps the inspiration for Captain Hook; in the next century the castle was burnt down. Much remains in spite of all this. Not far from the centre is a substantial stud, with around 150 horses; it's open to the public, and makes an original expedition. This interesting little site with its twenty-five pitches is an easy drive from St Malo, surely the most photogenic of the cross-channel ports and one worth visiting whether you're catching a ferry or not. The old town (which is not old at all, having been rebuilt after the last war) is like a walled fortress, a warren of little streets with some excellent shops and every imaginable variety of eatery. The rest of the town is a series of bays and coves, with beautiful views whichever way you look. The river Rance runs inland from here, and is a find in itself. Stay here and be well-placed for all this, and well-placed for crossing (and exploring) the whole of northern Brittany.

☎ **02 96 31 01 71**

---

50 *Manor house camping on a*
prehistoric site.
Manoir de Bonteville, Montours.

A wonderful place for lovers of history and fine buildings, well placed for exploring the north coast too. There are twenty-five pitches for camping here at the Manoir de Bonteville, which is four or five hundred years old at least – you can have a guided tour of it. The past thirty years have been spent unearthing (literally) history; there's a little museum of prehistory, where archeological treasures dating back millenia are on display; a relatively recent (tenth century) monastery and (positively ultra-modern) Gothic and Renaissance architecture to be seen too. Fifteen kilometres away is the mediaeval town of Fougères, whose castle, with its thirteen towers, is one of the most massive in Europe. Lovers of walking in woodlands will enjoy the fine beech forest that stretches out to the north-east of the town; dolmens and megalithic stones to find here too. Back at the manor, there are spectacular views over the countryside, lakes, birds and perfect peace. The coast, Mont St Michel, Granville, Cancale and some fifteen beaches are within an hour's drive.

☎ **02 99 95 16 60**

51 *A friendly farm with an auberge restaurant.*
La Maison Neuve, Chauvigne.

A little auberge on a farm where you'll get a warm welcome – literally, if you arrange to come in winter, when you can eat in the restaurant in front of the fire. This is a working farm, with lots of animals to see, which also serves traditional cuisine to its camping and B&B guests. Specialities, we're told, are nettle soup and ham on the bone. Ten pitches, lots of space and all sorts of outdoor activities on site, including canoeing, mountain biking, fishing, archery and boules. Wonderful walking country, and there's a riding centre nearby too. Real explorers should turn their backs on the coast for a while and visit Rennes, Brittany's capital – you're on the road to it here. It's a handsome city, its original mediaeval streets rebuilt in the Classical style with wide, Paris-style avenues, thanks to the efforts of a drunken carpenter who burnt down the old ones by mistake in 1720. There's a wonderful Museum of Brittany, and a fine cathedral (its predecessor survived the great fire but collapsed anyway). Make sure your journey between here and the farm takes you through the Forest of Rennes (it should, with minimal planning) and you'll find lovely paths through oak, beech, pine, birch and chestnut trees. After which, you'll need a good meal at the auberge!

☎ 02 99 95 05 64 *OPEN ALL YEAR*

52 *Breton culture and Breton friendship.*
Le Lot á Rieux, near Redon.

"At our little site we love having people who are interested in the history and the culture of our land. There's no luxury – just the necessary; washing and toilet facilities and a room for shelter if it's needed. We love recounting the story of our region, and often we go and chat to the campers. We play them the local music, and we help them to discover our heritage. We're also a walking centre; people can take paths leading straight from the site. We give them maps so they don't get lost. With friendly greetings from Brittany!" Nothing we could write could sum up this little place better than the letter the owners wrote to us. Monsieur and Madame le Villoux have thirteen pitches – "the camping's in an orchard, where it's quiet and cool – happiness!" they say. The river Vilaine is only half a kilometre away; this is the beautiful 'land of three rivers' (and one canal, the busy and picturesque Nantes à Brest). Nearby Redon manufactures cigarette lighters and is famous for its chestnuts; eels, cider and duck are other local specialities for the *explorer gastronomique*. Camp here, and make the most of a rare to chance to find out about the old Britanny; learn new things and make new friends. You may even learn to speak Breton, or play the bagpipes.

☎ 02 99 91 90 25

Breton

53 *Camping and riding beside the Loire.*
St Georges, Gennes.

A campsite attached to a horseriding school on a farm, two kilometres from the Loire in a lovely area for exploring whether you're a rider or not. A quiet little spot with twenty-five pitches, with free tennis, fishing and boules, and a play area for children; this is excellent walking country, and there are bikes to hire at the site too. Down by the river you can canoe, sail or simply watch the boats go by. As far as the horses are concerned, courses and sessions at every level are on offer, with a qualified instructor – everything from 'discovering' to 'perfecting', says the leaflet. Give Monsieur and Madame Loiseau a ring in advance if you want to do anything more than basic 'discovering' – they'll happily book you in for anything from an hour to a year. Experts and beginners alike can go out trekking – there are routes suited to all levels of expertise, and endless things to see. Troglodyte dwellings, forests, megalithic stones, chateaux dating back to the eleventh and twelfth centuries and the lovely Loire valley countryside all waiting to be explored, whether you're on two legs, four legs, two wheels or four. This is, of course, wine-making country – you can visit the cellars and taste the produce. Maybe 'perfecting' means learning to ride back in a straight line afterwards!

☎ **02 41 57 94 76 (phone and fax)**

54 *In the heart of vineyard country.*
Loire Country Holidays, near Saumur.

The access to this little six-pitch site is down a road lined with grapevines – red grapes on the right and white ones on the left. This is the heart of the Loire valley's best vineyard country; there are chateaux all around, including a very pretty one in the village, Montreuil Bellay, two kilometres away. The Butterfield family live here, and extend a warm invitation to campers looking for a serene base from which to explore the Loire valley; here you'll be private and secluded, looking over woodland to the river beyond. Explorers going out and about from here will find wine everywhere; there are marked 'wine routes' to follow, vineyards to visit and lots of opportunities to buy wine at the roadside. There's a fascinating 'Maison de Vin' in Saumur which makes a good starting-point for understanding how it's all done. Saumur has a great deal more to offer too. Its famous castle towers over the town, which has labyrinths of tiny streets and a fine tree-lined avenue along by the river. This is sparkling wine territory; you can visit the plant where a famous brand is made and learn about the 'méthode champenoise'.

☎ **02 41 38 74 17 Fax 02 41 50 92 83**

Foreign Fields

55 *Little site for visiting the big city.*
La Guillonniere, Beaumont-la-Ronce.

A simple little site which makes an ideal stopping-off point if you're travelling near Tours – just six pitches, and open all the year. A farm site, with produce to buy and breakfast available by arrangement, on the edge of the great expanse of forest which stretches to the south and west to Tours and beyond. Good territory for walking, cycling and generally recovering from long journeys, close to the might Loire and all its glorious chateaux and the little Loir with its own more modest but still considerable charms. Take the back roads from here to Tours and you'll find some pretty little places, including one called 'Hard-boiled Eggs'. There's probably an explanation of this somewhere, though not necessarily. Tours is very big and very busy; it has a railway station the size of a chateau, a masterpiece in the Baroque Monstrosity style. There are old streets and tiny lanes to wander around, and endless shops – a good stocking-up place for further travels. Follow the river and cross the forest to Chinon, one of France's most visited towns, and justifiably so.

☎ 02 47 24 42 83   •OPEN• ALL YEAR

---

56 *A friendly Loire Valley vineyard.*
Jocelyne et Rémi Desbourdes, near
Chinon.

A very friendly little site on a Chinon vineyard which produces Appelation Controllée Val de Loire wines, where campers are welcome to explore the farm, visit the cellars and the 'chai' (production/storage area; translates unromantically as 'shed'), taste the wines and buy some to take home (if the corks stay in that long!). There are farm products to be had, too – eggs, poultry, fresh garden vegetables, home made preserves – this is a site for lovers of French country life and French country food. Devotees of goats' cheese can make a pilgrimage to Ste Maure, fifteen kilometres away, the capital of the white crumbly substance (which has an Appelation Controllée system of its own). Bread to go with it can be found in the boulangerie

just up the road in the village, which has one other shop and a bar; there are walks in all directions from the site, which has just six pitches, so you won't be squashed. Lovers of fairy-tale chateaux will be absolutely torn between Chinon in one direction and Azay le Rideau in the other. Visit both and argue about it over a bottle of wine back at the farm.

☎ 02 47 95 24 30 Fax 02 47 95 24 83

57 Wine-growing family with a welcome for families.
Camping Caillé, near Chinon.

The Caillé family (Guy, Evette, Francois and Claude) have fifteen pitches on their wine-producing farm in Loire valley chateau-hunting country. This is a good site if you're travelling with small explorers; there's a good play area with swings and lots of room for careering around. There's ping-pong too (an amazingly good cure for the too-long-in-the car syndrome) and petanque, with tennis, mini-golf and a swimming pool just two kilometres away. The river's close by (La Vienne); there are lots of good walks, and lots of 'produits de la ferme', which in this case are liquid and come in bottles. Castles wherever you look round here, of course. The great chateau-building boom started with the wave of euphoria which followed the booting-out of the Brits in the fifteenth century. The style certainly owes more to Latin romanticism than to English solidity; explorers who detect a certain frilly femininity about some of the buildings will not be surprised to learn that women had a good deal of say in the design of several of them.

☎ **02 47 58 53 16 (phone and fax)**

58 Farm by the coast – with animations!
Le Ragis, Challans.

Monsieur Guyon's site is, he says, like no other campsite. It's right by the coast, and on a working farm – you can wander around it, and every morning there are eggs, milk, cheese, vegetables and bread to buy. Breakfasts are available, and so are table d'hote meals. You can walk or cycle to the eminently explorable coast, and discover the offshore islands, the fine sandy beaches and the strange marsh country. What indisputably makes it different is the remarkable energy Monsieur Guyon puts into making sure you're not bored. He sent us an astonishing programme of what he describes as 'animations', all of which are free. On Sunday, for example, he'll show you round the farm and face-paint the kids; then there's a clown (possibly Monsieur Guyon again). On Monday there's a boules contest; Tuesday's market day in Challans followed by nocturnal swimming, on Wednesday there's a walk to a menhir, on Thursday a fishing competition, on Friday a tour by car of the marshes. All this interspersed with 'animated evenings'. Monsieur Guyon assures us that the site's 'très calme', however, and although it's big by our standards (sixty pitches) it's certainly a fine example, we feel, of imaginative camping!

☎ **02 51 68 08 49 (phone & fax)**

•OPEN•
ALL YEAR

Foreign Fields

59 *Camp on a hill overlooking the Vendée.*
Peter and Jean Grant, near Pouzauges.

Peter and Jean Grant are campers themselves, and are delighted to welcome walkers, cyclists and small-tent campers to stay in their orchard (no access, alas, for vehicles, except possibly small motorhomes – ring and check). They live in the Vendée, in a house on a hill; from the site there are lovely views all round. A useful stopover site, or a place to linger and enjoyed well-signposted walks over wooded hills, birdwatching or simply a little serenity. A two-mile wander takes you to the village, which, with its watermill and ancient crooked bridge over a river in which you can swim, is particularly pretty – it has a shop, a bar and a boulangerie. Not much further and you're in the little market town of Pouzauges, where mod cons include a supermarket, restaurants, a pleasure lake and a leisure centre. Out and about you'll spot the windmills for which the region is famous – Moulin de Justice, in its beautiful setting, is open to the public; it sells its stone-ground flour and cakes and has a restaurant. The river Sevre has picture-book towns and is navigable by canoe. A friendly place to camp in a little-known and very special area.

☎ 02 51 92 81 03

---

60 *In the hills overlooking the Vendée.*
Peter and Chris Woodman, La Chataignerie.

Drive through the old farm courtyard and into Peter and Chris Woodman's two-acre meadow and you'll find you've arrived in a super little spot. They live in the lovely hills of the 'Bocage Vendéen', a patchwork of little hedged fields and woodland; there are extensive views of it from the meadow which, as you can see from the picture, has plenty of space and tranquility for six pitches. This beautiful area has an intriguing character of its own, with history and traditions to unearth and odd corners to explore. Escape from the car here; there are villages with bars and cafes only minutes away, and the quiet roads and plentiful paths make this excellent walking and cycling country. Close by

are the forest and lakes of Mervent/Vouvant and the timeless 'Venise Verte'.
Or go further afield; over by the sea La Rochelle has ramparts and an interesting harbour, and in season bustles with life; follow the coast south to Rochefort, a naval-dockyard town built rather somberely on a 'grid' layout, but with a past and a character of its own. Peter and Chris's site is one of our 'back garden' ones – not commercial developments, simply homes where families, sometimes French and sometimes people who've moved here from elsewhere, enjoy meeting people. Camp with them, and discover France through the eyes of the people who live there.

☎ 02 51 87 44 82

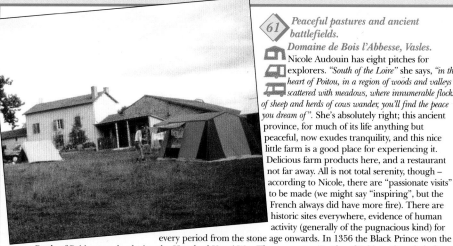

61 Peaceful pastures and ancient battlefields.
Domaine de Bois l'Abbesse, Vasles.

Nicole Audouin has eight pitches for explorers. *"South of the Loire"* she says, *"in the heart of Poitou, in a region of woods and valleys scattered with meadows, where innumerable flocks of sheep and herds of cows wander, you'll find the peace you dream of"*. She's absolutely right; this ancient province, for much of its life anything but peaceful, now exudes tranquility, and this nice little farm is a good place for experiencing it. Delicious farm products here, and a restaurant not far away. All is not total serenity, though – according to Nicole, there are "passionate visits" to be made (we might say "inspiring", but the French always did have more fire). There are historic sites everywhere, evidence of human activity (generally of the pugnacious kind) for every period from the stone age onwards. In 1356 the Black Prince won the Battle of Poitiers nearby during the Hundred Years' War. There were two Battles of Poitiers, though, before his; one in 507 when Clovis turfed out the Visigoths and one in 732 when Charles Martel meeted out the same treatment to the Arabs, thereby giving his name to a make of brandy. At Nicole's little campsite, though, there's a warm welcome for everyone.

☎ 05 49 69 03 46

62 Sheep and reality, virtual and otherwise.
Ferme de la Raudiére, near Poitiers.

Francois, Sylviane and the three little Girards would love you to come and camp with them on their farm near Poitiers – they opened their camp site (twenty-five pitches) the year before last, and are working hard to build it up. They've planted lots of trees since they took this photo of some of their early visitors. As you can see, this is a relaxed place where the campers and the farm get cheerfully mixed up together; there are meadows and cornfields all around, and usually farm produce to buy. The village of Latillé is just a kilometre away, and with 1400 inhabitants it's big enough to have shops for most things you're likely to need. A little river passes through it; its shaded

banks provide lovely walks and spots for fishing. Down the road is 'Sheep Village', a rather eccentric mini-theme park with sheep as superstars – not as daft as it sounds, reports a French newspaper. Pretty daft, all the same – but lots of fun. Much grander is world-famous Futuroscope, twenty-five kilometres away, a multi-million pound theme park about films, moving images, technology, virtual reality and the like. Monsieur Girard describes this as 'the big attraction of the region". We're not sure that the very real reality of camping on his little farm in the cornfields isn't a bigger one.

☎ 05 49 54 81 36

Foreign Fields

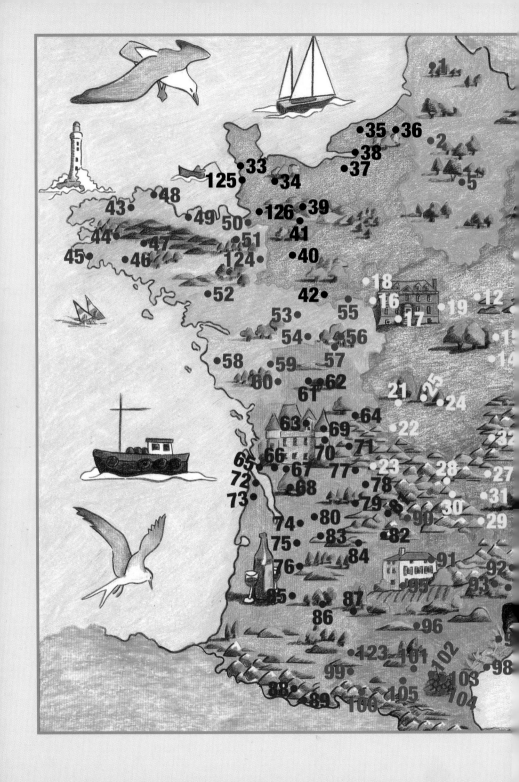

63 *Mills, rivers, marshes and markets. Le Moulin de Treneuillet, Chef-Boutonne.*

Two escaped teachers from England run this little site (thirty-two pitches), which is about three kilometres from the market square of the beautiful little town of Chef-Boutonne, source of the Boutonne river which runs along the southern boundary of the site. The river's narrow and shallow here, and very pretty. Camp around an ancient mill, and enjoy this peaceful countryside; lovely forests, easy walking and plenty of fishing. The chateau in the picture is just down the road at Javarzay, which also has a lovely church, some parts of which are eight hundred years old – it was once a Benedictine priory. Follow the 'Goats' Cheese Route' and meet goat-breeders and cheesemakers, or track down the local silver mine. Real explorers will be in their element in the Marais-Poitevin, a good portion of which has never been explored at all. Do it by boat to appreciate the silent, mysterious atmosphere of its myriad little canals. The marsh-dwellers are quiet people, with the air of a race apart; they build their low, white houses on islands of dry land and transport themselves and their livestock by boat. Wander from the site to the town and you'll find all that you need; the Saturday market sells everything from oysters and local cheese to sewing machines and winemaking equipment. A super little site with a wealth of interest all around.

☎ **05 49 29 73 46 (phone and fax) or 05 49 29 77 38.** OPEN ALL YEAR

64 *Warm Scottish hospitality in the Vienne valley.*
Le Peyrat Ecosse, near Millac.

Bungy-jumpers will love it here; from this aqueduct you can bounce to your heart's content. Those who prefer their terra a bit firma should take refuge at 'Le Peyrat' just up the road. In fact, it's called 'Le Peyrat Ecosse', in honour of the native land of Hilda and Alan, who own it and love living here. This is a little six-pitch corner of quiet and calm in the five-acre grounds of their 1930's farmhouse, where you're most welcome to stop and rest awhile. Lots of wildlife lives here, but it's well-behaved and won't disturb your tranquility, says Hilda; there are lovely walks along the banks of the river Vienne, horseriding, some nice cycle routes and plenty of good fishing. Lovely drives along it too – go north or south along its course and you'll find yourself on scenic roads. The village – L'Isle Jourdain – has canoeing, boating, water-ski-ing and a deer farm (as well as the bungy-jumping – this is a place definitely bordering on the eccentric). Good restaurants and an ample supply of bars. The welcome's warm here; take yourself off the main road and into the Vienne; discover a friendly site and a little place with character.

☎ **05 49 84 50 88** OPEN ALL YEAR

65 *Auberge camping across the estuary from the Médoc.*

Monsieur and Madame Roy.

An orderly farm site in the grounds of an auberge serving good country food. Nor far from the sea; about five kilometres to the coast and ten to a good beach, quickly covered on a bike in this flat estuary country near the mouth of the Gironde. This is the best bit of coast in the whole area; Talmont, just down the road, is particularly pretty and much visited. Here you're looking across to the Médoc; at Blaye, a little further down towards Bordeaux, there's a car ferry across. Worth an expedition northwards up the coast road, too; there are spectacular beaches and views to match along the stretch between Meschers and St Georges. Town explorers certainly shouldn't miss Royon. Once an elegant town of 1920s/1930s villas, it was just about annihilated in World War Two. The rebuilding, in that concrete-box style that seems to be common to all post-war port rebuilding in France, may be less characterful, but it's created a town of wide avenues and pleasant open spaces – and the beach and harbour around which it curves are stunning. Twenty-five pitches on the site, and plenty of essential shade - it gets hot down here!

☎ **05 46 90 70 31 (phone and fax)**

---

66 *Overlooking vineyards in the Cognac country.*

Richard and Lynn Day, near Gémozac.

Richard and Lynn live here in an eighteenth-century farmhouse and look out over vineyards; the lanes around them are lined with sunflowers in season, and from roadside stalls you can buy Charentais melons. Cheap local wine can be bought from local farms. The huge advantage of staying on one of these little private-house sites is that your hosts, who generally have only six pitches or less, have time (and the interest) to tell you all you need to know about their little patch – then you feel you've REALLY experienced it. Over and over again we hear "our customers have become friends".

Richard and Lynn will tell you that the best market is the one in Gémozac (four kilometres) on Fridays, where you can buy excellent local fish; that you can buy asparagus from the farm next door; that there are sandy coves nearby which are perfect for children. They'll tell you too about cognac – you're not far from the town of that name here (which has interesting distillery tours but alas is not beautiful). The brandy to which it gave its name was once made on the farms – many of the old farmhouses have a 'chai' running along the back in which the brandy was stored, and a few still have the old copper 'alambic', or still. Just as typical of the region – and more original - is pineau, a sweetish concoction invented by the accidental mixing of brandy and yet-to-be-distilled wine; it's addictively drinkable. There are five pitches here – basic facilities, but a very warm welcome.

☎ **05 46 94 15 16** •OPEN• ALL YEAR

67 *A little bit of an old world.*
Camping Chardon, near Pons.

This is a place where you'll know you've found a little corner of old France! Monsieur Talbot's farm is unsophisticated; the world of modernisation has passed him by, about which he's mightily relieved. Camp in his orchard, or maybe under a pine tree; there are twenty-one pitches, theoretically at least. The owners will be glad to see you; they'll organise a morning delivery of bread for you, and there's a bell so that you can call them 'day or night'. You'll notice here, and elsewhere in this region, that the farmhouses are on a grand scale, often with walled courtyards entered through great stone arches. In the days when the dreaded virus wiped out many of France's vineyards, the cognac producers grew very rich – their product, which of course they'd long had in storage, commanded high prices in a wine-deprived country. They spent their 'nouveau' money on grand farmhouses, many of which functioned, behind their walls, like little towns, making their own bread and raising their own livestock. Protestant households, excluded from the Catholic cemeteries, buried their dead under yew trees within the 'compound'. Time has faded the grandeur of the buildings and rusted the tractors, but the soul-restoring serenity of the simple country life is still in the air at this little site.

☎ 05 46 94 04 86

68 *In the garden of a cognac distillery.*
Madame Cellou, near Jonzac.

Camp in front of this Charentaise farmhouse, completely surrounded by vines. The farmhouse is also a distillery – they make wine, cognac and the delectable local liqueur, pineau – and you can explore the farm, visit the buildings, watch the process and see how it's done. Needless to say, you can taste and buy the end result, too; happily, it's a short stagger back across the path to the campsite. Madame Cellou is licensed for five or six pitches (a maximum of eighteen people), and she points out that she's always pretty full in July and August – outside this peak period, she says, it's much more peaceful, with more time for 'convivialité! If you're sober enough, there's trout fishing nearby, and some wonderful walks with ancient churches to discover. Wander into

nearby Jonzac and you'll find a pretty little town, which makes its living these days from brandy, barrel-making and, incongruously, butter. Explorers with a taste for the remote may enjoy the strange flat coastal country looking across the estuary to the Médoc; drive across through Mirambeau, under the motorway, round the particularly-pretty little patch of vineyards near Semoussac and out to Port-de-Cônac.

☎ 05 46 48 05 21

69 *Organic farm with meals and produce. Ferme de la Chassagne, near Villefagnan.*

Monsieur Peloquin describes the countryside around his organic farm as 'luminous', a quality which he's captured beautifully in this photo of it, surrounded with its golden cornfields. There are twelve pitches here, a swimming pool, canoeing (not on the swimming pool), free bikes and children's games. You can eat here too, wholesome country food – table d'hote dinner is sixty-five francs, breakfast twenty-five francs. Each week the Peloquins organise a communal meal made with their farm produce – see inside back cover! Plenty of organic produce to buy, and on the farm a little workshop where vegetables are dried and sunflower oil is produced (as well as the golden cornfields there are golden sunflower fields; cycling around the lanes lined with them must be one of the loveliest of France's simple experiences). You're welcome to go and watch it all, and to join in with the harvest too if you wish, in July. Son François is in charge of tourist information, and speaks English – there are chateaux and dolmens, archeological digs, museums, churches, forests and much more to discover. A particularly welcoming place, where you really can experience French farming life.

☎ 05 45 29 55 87   •OPEN• ALL YEAR

70 *Tents and bikes on the road south through Angoulême.*

La Maison Rosé, near Mansle.

Mr and Mrs King's little site by their pink house has six pitches for tents, in the middle of lovely touring country between Ruffec and Angoulême – from here you're within easy reach of Bordeaux, La Rochelle and Futuroscope, the amazing theme park near Poitiers. The roads are open and quiet, and the tourist office in nearby Mansle always has maps and route plans available, with organised walks and cycle trails in summer. Worth exploring the banks of the river Charente near here; it's one of France's loveliest rivers, and the stretch to the north of Mansle is one of the best. Or take the long straight main route into ancient Angoulême, named after eels (and capital of cartoons – there's a superb museum here on the subject). Well placed for travelling south, this is a cheery informal site, open in school holidays only and with a warm welcome for motorbike campers.

☎ 05 45 22 75 05

Foreign Fields

71 A tranquil corner in the lovely Charente.
La Blanchie, near Chabanais.

This little lady with the film-star looks and personal bodyguard is walking up the long land to 'La Blanchie', where Mrs Harris (her grandma) lives, and where there are twenty-five pitches for explorers in the midst of some of the loveliest countryside in the Charente. There are ten acres of pasture land here, and total privacy; the views are stunning. Walk, cycle, ride, go birdspotting or simply relax over a glass or two of Pineau. All essentials on site, with good access for disabled people; not far to go for local produce, shopping and eating. You're close to the river Vienne here; the little back road which follows it up to Confolens is particularly pretty, as are the riverside roads which follow it in the other direction all the way to Limoges – a lovely 'exploring' project for a lazy day, with a fascinating city at the end of the trail.

Look at the map and you'll see that there's an immense man-made lake just to the south, wonderful for swimming and messing about in boats. This is one of those sites where overnight stops turn into long stops – open all year, with other accommodation too, so pop in whenever you like!

☎ **05 45 89 33 19 (phone and fax)** •OPEN• ALL YEAR

---

72 *Motorcaravan camping on a Médoc vineyard.*
Chateau Sipian, Valeyrac.
We asked Monsieur Méhaye to send us a picture of something which conjured up the essence of his campsite, and he sent us his wine label. As his site is a 'Grand Vin de Bordeaux' chateau in the Médoc, we're inclined to agree that nothing conjures it up better. This is Chateau Sipian; there are six pitches, though we should warn you that they're for motor caravans with self-contained facilities only. The Méhaye family produce 150,000 bottles of wine a year, and very

CRU BOURGEOIS DU MEDOC

Grand Vin de Bordeaux

CHATEAU SIPIAN
MÉDOC

Vignobles MÉHAYE - Propriétaires

Tél. 56 41 56 05   33340 VALEYRAC   Fax 56 41 35 36

superior stuff it is too – taste it, take it home, drink it and remember your little tour in France. Touring the Médoc is huge fun, like driving through a wine list; famous name after famous name, all the way to Bordeaux. Pretty countryside too, not too hilly on the west side (if you've ever pictured yourself cycling through vineyards with the sun beating down on your back, this is the place to do it), thousands of acres of forest to the west with straight roads leading to the endless Atlantic beaches with their mighty breakers. A wonderful opportunity to stay on a vineyard in perhaps the most famous wine-producing region in the world.

☎ **05 56 41 56 05 Fax 05 56 41 35 36** •OPEN• ALL YEAR

73 Orchard of a private house.
Mrs Sharman, Lesparre - Médoc.

Next time you're meandering round the Médoc (and if you hadn't planned to you should) pop in and see Mrs Sharman. She lives just off the main road through the middle of this hallowed peninsular. This is her house; she has an orchard where up to six parties of explorers are welcome to camp. Visit the vineyards and chateaux, ride, cycle and walk – there are beautiful woodland walks on the doorstep, and for provisions Lesparre, with its two supermarkets, is only a couple of miles away. Take the car and wander past St-Estéphe, Chateau Lafite and Chateau Mouton Rothschild (buying wine in the supermarket will never be the same again) to Pauillac, a pretty pleasure port with lovely views across to the Gironde. Meander along a lovely stretch of road to Lamarque, from where the boat takes you across to Blaye on the 'mainland'. Blaye is a striking place, a lively port with views across the water from its magnificent 'citadelle' – there's a wonderfully French (and very contorted) nineteenth-century scandal featuring a duchess in an interesting condition, a chimney and a vain and villainous general. Make your way into Bordeaux, or go back to the site and potter lazily through the forests or off to the coast, with the prospect of a good bottle of wine to go back to – an excellent place to camp!

☎ 05 56 73 42 22　　•OPEN• ALL YEAR

74 On a vineyard near Saint Emilion.
Chateau Gerbaud, St Pey d'Armens.

Country camping in France is never expensive, but Madame Forgeat isn't much bothered about charging her campers at all – she says everyone who goes there buys wine from them. Which isn't surprising; this is their lovely old Bordelaise (Bordeaux-style) house with its vineyards and wine-storage buildings, just down the road (fifteen minutes by bike) from Saint Emilion. Motor caravans with all their own facilities only, alas – room for fifteen of them on a lovely piece of land, easy to find and easy to access. Saint Emilion is one of the most visited places in France, with good reason. It has a huge underground church carved into a cliff between the ninth and twelfth centuries – "the first impression when you enter is of profound astonishment and of a sort of religious awe which roots you to the spot" writes one visitor. It's a beautiful town, built in golden stone in the shape of an amphitheatre, with a particularly lovely market square. Pop into the tourist office and pick up a route plan for a tour of the Bordeaux vineyards, or explore Bordeaux itself. Busy traffic (and you may have to hunt for parking for a high vehicle), but it's splendidly pompous and eminently worth the detour – if you tire of the grand avenues, find the old town with its little back-street restaurants serving superb Bordeaux cuisine; try *magret de canard*, washed down with Armagnac.

☎ 05 57 47 12 39　Fax 05 55 70 47 20　　•OPEN• ALL YEAR　

Foreign Fields

75 *In a sea of vines by a Bordeaux chateau.*

Vignobles Bouchard, near Langon.

A warm welcome and free camping here for caravans and motor caravans needing no facilities. Spend a night or more in the middle of a sea of vines at Chateau Labatut, which sits on a hill overlooking the Garonne valley in the Première Côtes de Bordeaux area near Langon. Taste the wines (there's a beautiful reception area, with barrels of ageing wine stretching off into the distance) and carry some off to the campsite; these wines win prizes and gold medals. A third of the production here is exported, two thirds sold in France; try the 'Cadillac Liquoreux', which makes a wonderful apéritif. When you're ready to go exploring, you'll find you're on the Route of the Abbeys, just down the road from a mediaeval town and close to the tomb of Toulouse-Lautrec and his old house at St-André-du-Bois. Cadillac, after which the liqueur (not to mention the car) is named, is close by and has a splendid chateau built for dukes; at Sauternes there's the Chateau d'Yquem. Come when you want – the site can take ten or fifteen units and is open all year – but it's wise to phone if you plan to come at the weekend.

☎ **05 56 62 02 44 Fax 05 56 62 09 46** •OPEN• ALL YEAR

76 *Chateau with a restaurant between vineyards and Landes.*

Chateau d'Arbieu, Bazas.

This is the view, from the camping area, of the Château d'Arbieu – not a wine-making chateau, but one devoted entirely to good food and enjoying the natural environment. It's a lovely place to stay; there are only eighteen pitches in the enormous 'Great Meadow', so little explorers tired of touring vineyards will have plenty of room for leg-stretching. There's a pool here, a play area and bikes for hire. Charming Monsieur de Chenerilles has been working for sixteen years on turning this lovely building into a place to stay (he has B&B rooms here) and a place to eat – his 'chambre d'hote' restaurant is an excellent place to eat good country cuisine with fresh local ingredients.

He'll give you all the help you need to enjoy the area all around; the Saturday market in Bazas (twenty-five centuries old and worth exploring for a month of Saturdays) is a very good one, he says, and he knows where all the best farm produce is. He strongly recommends tucking into the grey beef cattle that you'll see wandering around; their meat he considers incomparable. Here you're between the Sauternes/Graves vineyards on one side and the magnificent Landes pine forests on the other; wander west a little, and you'll find the picturesque gorges of the river Ciron. Cycle or walk for miles and miles. A lovely place to stay.

☎ **05 56 25 11 18 Fax 05 56 25 90 52**

77 *Unspoilt nature and 'convivialité.*
La Ripole, Abjat sur Bandait, Périgord.

This is 'La Ripole' at Abjat sur Bandait, conker capital of France – see page fifteen! It's deep in lovely wooded hills; a little stream tumbles through it and this lovely lake is yours for fishing and swimming. The swimming's particularly welcome in summer, which is uncompromisingly hot; spring is warm and sunny, with cool evenings perfect for walking and riding. Often groups of campers go off on rambles together – this is a sociable site, with its thirty-two pitches, where there's always someone interesting to talk to. Sometimes there's a communal meal in the evening, often impromptu, with traditional Périgord food. Wander into the village (one of the most beautiful in France, and that's official) and you'll find friendly little shops and, of course, the famous English pub where the conker team train hard. Wander further and you'll find caves, chateaux, churches and museums. Make absolutely sure your wanderings take you to Brantôme, called the 'Venice of the Périgord' because of its waterways; it has a magnificent Benedictine abbey, cave dwellings, a museum of prehistory, chateaux and fine houses. Shady and cool with riverside walks, it's atmospheric and beautiful.

☎ **05 53 56 86 85/05 53 56 38 81**

78 *By the side of a watermill on the road to Thiviers.*

Le Touroulet, Thiviers, Dordogne.

Doris Norman's little site is, as you can see, in the loveliest of settings. By the side of an old watermill, there's a river on one side and woodland on the other; gloriously remote and rural though it looks, though, it's very close to the main road from Limoges to Périgeux – an ideal base if you're touring this deservedly popular part of France. You can swim in the lake here – there's even a beach – and there's a little restaurant offering home-cooked food. A one-kilometre walk takes you into the nearest village, which has all essential supplies, and twelve kilometres takes you into the town of Thiviers. This lively little place has been there since the days of the Gauls (Asterix et al); later pilgrims stopped here on the way to Santiago de Compostella in

Spain. The markets here are very famous, and you can buy foie gras and truffles. Explore also what is (probably) the world's only Duck and Goose Museum. People here are very fond of ducks and geese, in a culinary sort of way. Stock up with wonderful goodies, take them back to the site and eat them by the side of the lake with a bottle of wine. Bliss.

☎ **05 53 62 07 90**

79 Woodland peace near beautiful Périgeux.
Mr and Mrs Wilkinson, Le Bois de Coderc, Antonne-et-Trigonant.

Explorers here can enjoy the particularly appealing luxury of feeling themselves to be deep in the woods and far from civilisation, whilst at the same time being a stone's throw from a Relais Routier restaurant. One doesn't need to be a tough pioneering type ALL the time, after all. This is a supremely peaceful site, with the simplest of facilities; it's just on the edge, though, of the little village of Antonne-et-Trigonant, on the main road leading east from fascinating Périgeux. Among Périgeux's many monuments is an ancient pagan temple, eighty feet high and open to the sky, with a gap in its circular walls through which, we are told, a devil forced his way out when St Front turned up and tried to convert him to Christianity. The saint had better luck with the rest of the Périgord, though, and there's a very fine cathedral to prove it. You could walk around these pretty little streets for days and not tire of them; there are markets and little cafés, and mediaeval houses in abundance. Equally, explorers can find places near here that make Périgeux look modern; prehistoric sites and caves abound, the most famous of course being at Lascaux, to the south east. Back at the site you could try a spot of fishing or horseriding, or simply relax by the river – there are two little islands which can be reached on foot, to the delight of children.

☎ **05 53 06 00 65 Fax 05 53 05 99 48**

---

80 Animals, vineyards, history and the warmest of welcomes.
Jill and Peter Joiner, Guinet, Dordogne/Gironde border.

Always something to lean over a fence and chat to here – Jill and Peter keep sheep, goats, ponies, turkeys, ducks, pigs and chickens. Free dog hire too – always one of those that needs taking for a walk! They live on the border between the Dordogne and the Gironde (literally; the stream that flows through their bottom field IS the border). Camp here, close to wonderful Saint Emilion, surrounded by vines, woods and fields and with splendid views of a chateau – it's a happy, friendly place, with six pitches and masses of space, near a pretty little village with shops, two bars and a restaurant. Five minutes away is a lake where energetic explorers can swim, sail, ride or fish, while less energetic ones look on with glass in hand. Vineyards everywhere – this is the Dordogne/Bordeaux border, so the choice of wine is quite superb. History everywhere too; visit Castillon, site of the last battle of the Hundred Years' war (France 1, England 0). From here too you can easily reach Bordeaux, another place where English history and French have long mingled; this finest of cities was once the capital of Aquitaine, cunningly aquired by Henry Plantagenet when he married Eleanor of that province. Now it's gloriously, incontrovertibly French, almost as lively and stylish as Paris. Shop here in elegant avenues for sophisticated luxury goods – or go back to the site and buy Jill and Peter's vegetables, eggs, home-cured bacon and home-made sausages. A really super place to stay.

☎ **5 53 80 72 13 Fax 05 53 81 68 95** *OPEN ALL YEAR*

81 *In the grounds of a Périgord manor house.*
Hamelin-Périgord-Vacances, St Amand
de Coly.

Monsieur Hamelin enthusiastically invites you to come and camp in the grounds of his sixteenth-century manor house in the magical Périgord Noir – there are seventy-five acres of meadows and woodland here, so no need to worry about overcrowding! The buildings (as you can see) are lovely, and so is the setting; it's sunny, unspoilt and peaceful (apart, that is, from the cicadas, which are pretty enthusiastic serenaders). It's the sort of site where you feel genuinely welcome, a friendly family place with a happy atmosphere. Monsieur Hamelin is particularly proud of the enormous number of things there are to see and do near here; he sent us a wonderful map (also reproduced on the back of his envelope) plastered with 'curiosités', together with impressive calculations as to how many there were and how many would be open on given days of the week. The conclusion seems to be that there are between forty and eighty places to visit close by – caves, chateaux, grottos, museums and more – of which a minimum of thirty-seven would be open on any one day. To which you should add the one hundred beaches; as you can see, this is serious exploring territory. It would be tempting, of course, to sit on the site in the sun, contemplating the centuries-old buildings, watching odd animals potter around and deciding which bottle of wine to open for supper.

☎ **05 53 51 68 59/05 53 51 60 64**

82 *Site in the centre of the sights.*
La Ferme le Grel, Domme, Dordogne.

Lovely Dordogne-style buildings, the home of Derek and Doris Williams, who have room in this green meadow for eight pitches; they also offer breakfasts and table d'hote meals at very good prices. They live in a particularly lovely bit of this popular area, close to the Dordogne river and to prime tourist areas such as Sarlat-la-Caneda and Rocamadour – if you want to be centrally-placed for touring, this is an ideal base for you. Just two kilometres away (walk or cycle if you can; it's too pretty round here for whizzing past in cars) is Domme, considered the most beautiful hilltop village of them all, golden, picturesque and with stunning views. It's seven hundred-and-something years old (at least). Wherever you are in the Périgord you'll find yourself surrounded by the wonderful food for which it's renowned. The greatest of the regional delicacies of course is the revered truffle, credited with aphrodisiac qualities; looking like a small black clod of earth, it is in fact a sort of subterranean mushroom, spending its days living off the roots of trees until being rooted up by a pig (or these days, a dog) and sold for a king's ransom. Possibly one has to be French to understand what all the fuss is about; there seems to have been more written about the cooking of truffles than about liberté, egalité and fraternité put together. Geese feature a great deal on menus, and this is walnut country par excellence.

☎ **0044 151 6088119 (book via UK agents please)**

83 Views over picturesque valleys in southern Dordogne.
Mirathon, near Duras.

A pretty site with valley views and a water garden, where you can enjoy a barbecue or a swim in the pool. 'Mirathon' is near Duras, in the southern part of the Périgord region. It's easily found, not too far from the main road into Ste Foy la Grande in the Dordogne valley; prettier, though, than this road, if you have time, is the patch of countryside you'll cross if you go from here to Bergerac on the back roads. Bergerac is very much worth a detour; it's excellent for provisions, particularly if you go on a market day, and the hustle and bustle of this busy commercial town (it makes its living largely from tobacco these days) is a nice contrast to the quiet of the countryside. Cyrano, its best-known citizen, had very little to do with the town (if anything at all) until his exploits (and his nose) became famous, at which point this detail was overlooked and he was installed on a pedestal with immense civic pride. Another expedition worth mounting takes you to Eymet, a beautiful bastide town where you can buy wonderful plums (you're very close the great plums-and-prunes region around Agen here) and jams. Get out into the countryside on foot or wheels if you can; it's quite unspoilt here, and teems with wildlife. Festivals, fireworks, markets and events in abundance in this region; the site has an excellent reception area crammed with ideas and information.

☎ 05 53 83 08 47

84 Friendliness and fresh bread at Monsieur Pimouguet's mill.
Moulin de Mandassagne, near Villeréal.

This is Monsieur and Madame Pimouguet, making their country-style bread at their mill on the edge of the Lot region. "You'll be seduced (we hope) by our little site, with its family atmosphere" they say. This we don't doubt; you'll certainly be seduced by the flavour of the bread. Dearly as we all love the baguette, it's not the only bread in France, and the round rustic kind is high on flavour and keepability, with less of a tendency to glue itself firmly to the roof of your mouth; ask Monsieur Pimouguet. You should be able to track down some good plum jam to go with it in this area; there's farm produce on sale at the site, so they may even

have some. Real explorers of the sporty (or hot) variety can enjoy a swim in the pool; you can play tennis or master the mysterious business of boules. You're on the edge of lovely wooded countryside here, with quiet roads which are a cyclist's dream. Over to the east are the high, dramatic Lot gorges and some of the remotest and most atmospheric regions of the Massif Central; to the south is the Garonne valley, a fast communications corridor linking the Mediterranean and the Atlantic. From this happy and interesting little site you could explore the whole of south-west France- and eat good bread, too!

☎ 05 53 36 04 02 (phone and fax)

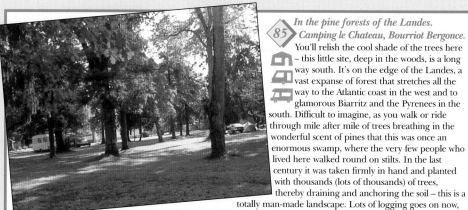

In the pine forests of the Landes.

85 *Camping le Chateau, Bourriot Bergonce.*
You'll relish the cool shade of the trees here – this little site, deep in the woods, is a long way south. It's on the edge of the Landes, a vast expanse of forest that stretches all the way to the Atlantic coast in the west and to glamorous Biarritz and the Pyrenees in the south. Difficult to imagine, as you walk or ride through mile after mile of trees breathing in the wonderful scent of pines that this was once an enormous swamp, where the very few people who lived here walked round on stilts. In the last century it was taken firmly in hand and planted with thousands (lots of thousands) of trees, thereby draining and anchoring the soil – this is a totally man-made landscape. Lots of logging goes on now, and extraction of resin, much of which finds its way into detergent bottles – look out for things scented with 'pin des Landes' in the supermarket. From the site, owned by four very friendly English people, you can explore the dark depths of this strange country or the bright lights of Bordeaux. You might like to make your way over to the coast, an immense stretch of golden sand, much of it completely isolated; there are some resorts, though, and still some unspoilt villages – try Lit-et-Mixe, a particularly pretty example. By way of a real culture shock, the Gulf of Arcachon is a playground of the rich and fashionable; at least the oysters are cheap here. Hannibal types fancying a major expedition over the mountains could make it to Lourdes from here; it's depressingly Disneyfied, but an experience none the less.

☎ **05 58 93 36 22** •**OPEN**• **ALL YEAR**

86 *Woodland and vineyards in the Armagnac country.*
Rose d'Armagnac, near Montréal, Gers.
This little lad needed to walk just ten metres from one of the woodland pitches on this site to find his grapes – 'Rose d'Armagnac' is surrounded with them. There are plenty to spare for an odd nibble before they go off to be transformed into the brandy-like nectar after which the site is named. Armagnac has a rich, woody flavour, and is considered by many to be superior to the cognac competition; we recommend extensive research, either at one of the many local farms and distilleries which welcome visitors or in one of the fine restaurants for which the Gers is known. For this is Gascony, a land of very fine food and lots of regional specialities (but no place to be a duck). Around the site, and often on it, deer graze, sunflowers grow and the sun shines; there are twenty-two acres of land, and a little lake where you can fish. Two kilometres away, the typical bastide village of Montréal was built by the British, though it doesn't show; the Romans might reasonably argue that it was built by them first, as there are bits and pieces they left behind to be seen (and dug up) everywhere. A super place for lovers of history, lovers of nature and lovers of fine food and drink. At Condom you can cruise the canal, and at Auch you can see where Musketeer D'Artagnan lived – rumour has it that he was the ONLY musketeer. And from here an expedition to Spain is totally feasible – you can get there in two hours or so. A nice little thirteen-pitch site (English-owned), beautifully situated.

☎ **05 62 29 47 70 (phone and fax) (or UK agent: 00 44 1489 582413)** •**OPEN**• **ALL YEAR**

Foreign Fields

87 A pretty little patch of heaven on the pilgrims' route.
Ferme de Barrachin, near Lectoure.

"Come and eat with us, if you'd like to" say farmers Monsieur and Madame Esparbes, down in the Gers. *"You can camp in our shady meadow – there are cornfields, sunflower fields and vineyards all around. And for cooking your own meals, we can offer you poultry, lovely fresh eggs, fruit, vegetables and herbs from the kitchen garden – and wine, of course. You'll get a warm welcome here".* This is a peaceful and pretty little patch of heaven – eight pitches on a small farm near Lectoure. Walk for miles – people have been doing that for a long time here, right on the pilgrimage route to the shrine at Compostella in Spain, which in the Middle Ages was as celebrated a site as Rome and Jerusalem; thousands upon thousands of people, wearing the shell emblem which was the sign of their purpose, made the journey from all over Europe. Along the way they were lodged and looked after by the little communities through which they passed, and there are many traces to be seen even now of their travels, echoes of an age with very different values. Wander three kilometres into the little town of Lectour and you'll realise you've found something special. It's very beautiful, and steeped in the deep past; here you can see altars where bulls were sacrified in ancient rituals, and traces of the Gauls (and just about every civilisation since). Be stunned by the view of the Pyrenees from the garden near the town hall, and visit a reconstructed nineteenth-century chemist's shop. Lots of leisure facilities here too – all in all a fascinating place to explore.

☎ **05 62 68 84 57 Fax 05 62 68 97 32**

88 A thousand metres up in the Pyrenees.
La Pose, Estaing.

Pure, mountain air, sunshine, trout fishing, mushrooms, bilberries and edelweiss – these are the Hautes-Pyrenees, and this little site's a thousand metres up in them. A mountain stream runs through it; you can climb, seriously or otherwise, or simply walk the mountain paths, discover the wonderful flora and fauna and watch the flocks of sheep and goats high up on their summer pastures. Go down to the valley and you can play tennis, swim or ride on the edge of the lake. There are twenty-five pitches here, and fans of the niftily-named 'caravaneige' will be delighted to know that it's open all year for those in possession of good thermal underwear. Remote though it looks, the site is on a farm, which you're welcome to explore, and where you can buy farm produce (including wonderful honey from high-altitude bees); B&B's available, and there's a restaurant just a kilometre away. Fifteen kilometres takes you to the mountain resort town of Argelès-Gazost; this sheltered area along the river valley is thick with little villages and shrines in picturesque settings. Only thirty kilometres away is Lourdes (remember, when calculating journey times around here, to take the contour lines into account). The Lourdes pilgrimages started in 1873; in 1874 fourteen people made the journey in search of a cure. In 1993, five and a half million people went there.

☎ **05 62 97 10 11/05 62 97 43 10** •OPEN• ALL YEAR

Real

Exploring in **SOUTH WEST FRANCE**

89 *Up with the bears and the marmots.*
Les Tilleuls, near Gedre.

The Pyrenees National Park is home to bears, marmots and vultures; this spectacular kingdom in the clouds is a world of its own. Discovering its wildlife is made easy and enormous fun by the excellent National Park information centres, where serious zoologists and botanists can access detailed and scientific information. Smaller (or less serious) ones can meet Barnabé the bear, Samy the marmot, Achille the eagle, Hector the vulture and their various friends and acquaintances, which include vast flocks of migrating birds and a whole range of goat/antelope types.. If, that is, they can drag themselves away from the stunning views, the picturebook villages, the sunny pastures -and our little twenty-five pitch site, eleven hundred metres above sea level. Here live Monsieur and Madame Millet, near the village of Gedre in a lovely old Pyrenean farmhouse (where they have accommodation should you fancy a change from the great outdoors for a night or so). *"We love having overseas visitors – we have lots of Dutch friends here, for example – we really like that. I speak a little bit English with accent the Pyrenees ...!"*. Worth climbing quite a few Pyrenees to stay at this happy little place, where there are games to amuse the children, horseriding and lovely walks and all the help you need to enjoy your stay. No distance at all from Spain down here!

☎ 05 62 92 48 92

Foreign Fields

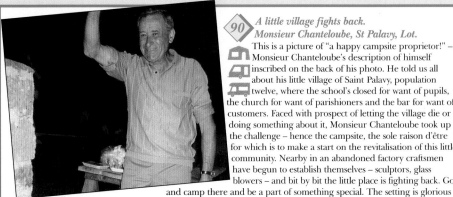

90 *A little village fights back.*
Monsieur Chanteloube, St Palavy, Lot.

This is a picture of "a happy campsite proprietor!" – Monsieur Chanteloube's description of himself inscribed on the back of his photo. He told us all about his little village of Saint Palavy, population twelve, where the school's closed for want of pupils, the church for want of parishioners and the bar for want of customers. Faced with prospect of letting the village die or doing something about it, Monsieur Chanteloube took up the challenge – hence the campsite, the sole raison d'être for which is to make a start on the revitalisation of this little community. Nearby in an abandoned factory craftsmen have begun to establish themselves – sculptors, glass blowers – and bit by bit the little place is fighting back. Go and camp there and be a part of something special. The setting is glorious (views over orchards and distant hills) and there are lovely places to visit all around, including the famous 'red' village of Collonges. There are ten pitches on the farm; you can learn to play boules here (competition every Friday night!) and to fire a bow and arrow. The site is part of the imaginative 'Taste of the Farm' scheme, providing you with a rare opportunity to try some of the old specialities of the region (don't miss the pastries). And don't go home without trying 'ratafia', an ancient drink traditionally consumed when a deal was concluded – or 'ratified'. Made from distilled wine spirit and grapejuice, it can (and should) be consumed before, during or after deals, meals or at any time whatsoever. Monsieur Chanteloube sent us mouthwatering pictures of his farm produce, his spit-roast barbecues – and the photo inside the back cover, of one of his 'friendly evenings'.

☎ **05 65 32 12 53**

91 *Quiet little site in dramatic Aveyron setting.*
'L'Occitan', Peyrusse-le-Roc

Here's a nice little site near a famous little site. Peyrusse le Roc is an ancient village perched dramatically on a rock, squabbled over since the seventh century at least. In spite of being repeatedly captured by the English, it never lost its loyalty to the French throne, for which fidelity eventually it was granted a royal charter conveying all sorts of privileges on its inhabitants. By the fourteenth century it reigned over 107 parishes, and supported grand families and exalted officials a-plenty. Its fortunes declined, though; in 1719 it lost its position as chief town of the region and its nobles and merchants abandoned it in search of richer pastures. It remains proud of it history, and you

can be shown round its streets by ladies and gentlemen of days gone by; on August 31 there's a spectacular festival of fireworks and music. This region is the Aveyron, high, remote and rocky with mountain rivers and dramatic gorges – an area thick with the little settlements of the past. Don't even try to cross it quickly – a wander round its little roads will take you back in time. Don't miss the valley of the river Lot winding its way to Entraygues, and the lovely gorges to the south on the way towards the (relatively) large town of Rodez. The Massif Central is famous for its dramatic thunderstorms; they're wonderful to watch, but be prepared.

☎ **05 65 80 43 32**

92 *Among the rocks in the Cevennes National Park.*

Madame Pantel, Pont de Montvert.

The Cevennes National Park, says Madame Pantel, is famous for its "chaos of blocks of granite". You'll see some of them in the picture; in fact, you can come and camp in between them. The Cevennes are famous for other things too; for their remoteness, for their trout fishing, for their provision of a refuge for the fleeing, persecuted Protestants of days gone by and for their spectacular beauty. This is an area where you can walk for mile upon mile, and hear nothing but silence. Our welcoming little site here is high in the mountains – the nearest peak is 1700 metres – and provides a tranquil base for touring; there's farm produce to buy and a village with all facilities and 'animations' just five kilometres away. Look out for the trout fishing, and also for the bilberry festival! Spectacular gorges and mountain drives just to the east of here. Twenty pitches, pure mountain air and some of France's truly wide open spaces.

☎ **04 66 45 81 82/04 66 45 82 16**

93 *Pretty farm site in the land of spectacular gorges.*

La Quillette, Rousses.

The little 'Quillette' campsite owes its name to the nearby mountain. This is the approach to the site, which sites on the banks of the river Tarnon on the edge of an oak forest, in the superb Cevennes National Park. Follow lovely waymarked walks in the woods, or fish in the river; take the car and explore some of the wildest and windiest roads in France. Try for example the 'Corniche des Cevennes', or go west to Meyrueis, which has managed to retain its down-to-earth working town character in spite of being stunningly pretty and pored over by thousands of tourists each year. Explore the Tarn gorges; drive along the river from Ste Enimie to Le Rozier and you'll be stunned by the scenery though possibly overwhelmed by the traffic too in high

season; try, if you can, to see this lovely river by boat (there are trips available, or you can canoe!). The campsite has twenty-five pitches and all you need to be comfortable and relaxed; there are wild fruits to find in the forest, and mushrooms to pick. A pretty corner of a remarkable region.

☎ **04 66 44 00 29**

Foreign Fields

94 Travels in the Cevennes (donkey optional).
Camping La Garde, near Florac.

Cross the glorious Cevennes in the footsteps of Robert Louis Stevenson and his donkey Modestine – his account of his journey, written in 1880, still inspires many walkers to do the same (with and without donkeys), scrupulously respecting every step and meander. *"I moved in an atmosphere of pleasure, and felt light and quiet and content. I have not often enjoyed a place more deeply ..."* he writes; come and enjoy it deeply yourself, at this romantic little site on a sunny slope between the village and a cascading river. As well as swimming in the clear blue river with its rocky outcrops, you can 'build dams' in it, and if you're not keen on donkeys you can explore in army jeeps; the photo shows some of the more rugged country, seen in the early morning mist. For a less arduous excursion, visit the 'Magnanerie de la Roque', where in a lovely setting you can learn about the silk industry, which in the thirteenth century made the Cévennes a rich area, thanks to mulberry bushes brought back from the Crusades. A rich area in conventional terms it certainly isn't these days, but it has a fabulous wealth of natural beauty, wildlife, architecture, atmosphere and character. The owners of 'Camping La Garde' are clearly totally infatuated with it all; so are their customers.

☎ **04 66 45 94 82 Fax: 04 66 45 95 18**

95 Out and about from a tiny riverside site.
La Camperie du Cande, Lapenche.

Six quiet pitches in the shade, surrounded by flowers and on the banks of a river – this is a super little spot if you're down in the Midi-Pyrénées. Room for children to play and games to play with, a 'relaxation area' by the river and scope for fishing. One of the beauties of touring this part of France is that the roads are so good; if you've come down from creeping round the hills of the Massif, or just want to cover a lot of ground quickly, you'll enjoy the fact that Tarn-et-Garonne is very well connected. Monsieur and Madame Rendier's farm site is only five kilometres from the RN20. The town of Caussade is a good base for provisioning expeditions, and Montauban, prettily built in pink brick and serving as the major market town for the delectable fruit and vegetables of the region, is an easy drive away. From here you can strike out in all directions and find all sorts of things – Carcassonne, film-set walled city on the banks of Canal du Midi, Rocamadour, perched improbably but impressively on its hill, the Bordeaux and Armagnac vineyards, gorges, caves and dramatic rivers. Absolutely essential to go to Albi (also pink) which has a colossal cathedral and a splendid museum dedicated to the work of its famous son, Toulouse-Lautrec; other masterpieces on display include one which is twenty thousand years old (or so).

☎ **05 63 31 96 51**

Real

96 *Cathars, castles and charming towns.*
La Rigaudie, Giroussens.

Monsieur Gaben points out that his site is within half an hour of Toulouse, Albi, Castres and Cordes; he also supplies an impressive list of ideas for day trips and half-day excursions. Don't leave, he says (in capitals) without doing the 'Wine Route'. Once sobererd up from that, there are local attractions at nearby Giroussens – an outdoor leisure centre, a riding school, a pottery, a little steam railway – and pretty villages to pop into, notably Lavaur (good Saturday market) and Montans, which invites you to visit its 'Archéoscope'. Bigger neighbour Gaillac hasn't got one of those, but it does have an enchanting riverside setting, pretty streets and squares, fountains and (next to the Abbey) a wine museum – the Gaillac vineyards, planted by monks around a thousand years ago, are an important part of this region's economy. Take yourself off to Verfeil and find a city of the Cathars, 'heretics' who fought long and hard for influence in this region; a serious threat to the establishment, they were ruthlessly exterminated in the thirteenth century. Traces of their culture (and their castles) survive all over the south west; their story is one worth exploring. Twenty-five pitches here, plus a warm welcome and lots of help and advice.

☎ **05 63 41 67 20**

---

97 *A working vineyard with a welcoming auberge.*
La Ferm de Pélicon, near Gignac, Hérault.

This is one of those lovely wine-making farms with a 'family' rather than 'big business' feel to it. This scene probably hasn't changed much since the hills were young and man first discovered that fermented grape juice had definite advantages over the raw sort. You're warmly invited to come and join in with it all. There are twelve pitches in a large, shady area of pine woodland, and the farm has an auberge restaurant too. It's beautifully quiet, yet only five minutes away is Gignac, which has all facilities and France's best eighteenth-century bridge – there's a viewing platform from which you can admire its 175 metres of splendid architecture. This is the valley of the river Hérault, which having plummeted down from the Massif Central wends its way more peacefully across this otherwise arid and very southern-looking plain to the Mediterranean. Wend your way there yourself, and discover ancient Sète with its bustle and fishing boats and little bars on the quay where you can watch the mighty tuna being loaded and eat mussel kebabs; explore the odd lagoon of the Bassin de Thau and find timeless Méze and its oyster beds. At Agde you can join the thousands who wander around with no clothes on; this is one of a handful of resorts along this coast, which is far less fashionable and far more interesting than its trendy counterpart the Cote d'Azur. Stay inland, and there are lakes, gorges and grottos, pretty towns like Pézenas and the splendid city of Montpellier. The REAL south of France, from a real working vineyard site.

☎ **04 67 57 68 92 (phone and fax)**

Foreign Fields

98 By the sea in a sea of vines. Domaine de Querelle, Serignan.

Camping by the Mediterranean – in the middle of a sea of vines! This super little farm site is on a hillside covered with vineyards just two kilometres from the coast. Soft golden sand (as you can see), and warm blue water – bathe from dawn to dusk if you like. Then wander back to the farm, buy a bottle or two of wine from friendly Monsieur and Madame Abel, and perhaps some of their honey and fresh vegetables, walk back to your pitch through the vines and contemplate the Mediterranean sunset. A night out on the town is easily arranged too, point out the Abels – all sorts of entertainments go on in nearby Valras and Serignan. By day you can explore the varied coast between here and the Spanish border. Arrive at Narbonne in the morning and visit its huge and truly wonderful covered market, the best in France – delicious food of every imaginable variety to buy here. Come back in the evening and you'll find its quays and bridges full of life. Continue down the coast past nature reserves and oil terminals, boring bits and beautiful fishing villages – take the little coast road for interest, the motorway for speed if you're off to Spain. Or for a different experience explore the enchanting Canal du Midi, following the towpath through timeless villages – find Capestang, Roubia, Paraza, Homps, Le Somail – and watch the boats go by from a canalside bar or restaurant. A little further (by towpath or motorway) and you reach Carcassonne, a spectacular walled city much used as a film set, and so perfect you wonder if it's real.

☎ **04 67 32 03 01**

99 A gourmet adventure chez Monsieur Perissas. Ferme de Preville, Boulogne-sur-Gesse.

This is the view from Monsieur Perissas's farm as the sun goes down over the hills; his site is, in his words, a little pocket of fresh air in a haven of tranquility. He has ten pitches, in an area shaded by poplars and pines, from which you can wander out into this lovely countryside on foot, by bike or by vehicle; you'll find rivers, lakes, hills and lovely views wherever you look. On one side is the Gers country, and on the other the contrasting landscape of the Hautes-Pyrénées. The site is right next to the village of Boulogne-sur-Gesse, which has shops and bars and also a swimming pool and a 'nautical centre'. On the farm, genial Monsieur Perissas, a Frenchman with his

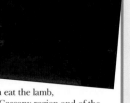

nation's firm ideas about what matters in life, has installed that essential ingredient for the *explorer gastronomique*, the auberge restaurant – here, he says, you can eat the lamb, poultry and vegetables he produces, and also all the traditional specialities of both the Gascony region and of the Pyrénées. This is after all, he says, the land of good living and good eating! He suggests you come along soon, for a gourmet adventure. Well, you can't explore France without exploring its menus, can you?

☎ **05 61 88 23 12 (phone and fax)**

100 Pizzas, bears and mountain passes. Monsieur Eambon, Col du Portet d'Aspet.

A wonderful place for lovers of mountains, pizzas, pot-holing and the Tour de France. Monsieur Eambon's little site (twenty-five pitches) is on a mountain pass, 1070 metres up in the Pyrenees, not very far at all from the Spanish border. Those of us who puff up barely perceptible inclines will be awed to learn that this is on the Tour de France route. It's also near Andorra, surely Europe's oddest country, a little kingdom of tax-free shops; the vertiginous approach road is thick with lorries driving hundreds of perilous miles to deliver goods to its centre, followed by cars making the same journey to buy them and bring them out again. Worth visiting, though, for the serious mountain scenery and so that you can say that you've been there. Just a few kilometres from here the shy mountain bears of the Pyrenees have been spotted; birds of prey abound. There are wonderful rambles from here along the pass, and, should you tire of the scenery above ground, there's a whole world of caves and potholes into which you can plunge. When you surface, park yourself outside Monsieur Eambon's little café-bar and recover with a pizza, or amble the two hundred metres down the road where there's a restaurant.

☎ 05 61 96 13 16

101 Camping at a lakeside auberge. Le Cathare, near Castelnaudary.

This is the dining room of the Auberge Le Cathare, a very civilised place to spend an evening after a day's exploration. The outside of this renovated little hotel, with its walled garden, makes a lovely photograph too. Attached to it is a super little twenty-five pitch site, where you can camp in quiet parkland full of trees, many of which are over a hundred years old. There are children's games, mini-golf and boules. The whole ensemble overlooks an immense and very beautiful man-made lake, where you can swim, sail and fish – the outlook, and the walks, are lovely. The auberge serves traditional country cuisine, including regional specialities; you can also order dishes to take away, and buy farm produce. An expedition of the gastronomic variety not to be missed from here is a visit to Castelnaudary, world capital of cassoulet. Take yourself off to this canalside town when you're very hungry and enjoy one of the best peasant dishes in the world (then look for the canned version with 'Castelnaudary' on in the supermarket – just about as good). Look out, when you explore this region, for the ruined hilltop castles of the Cathars.

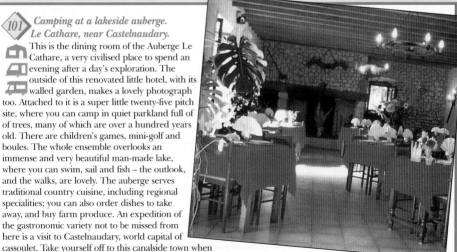

☎ 04 68 60 32 49 Fax 04 68 60 37 90

Foreign Fields

102 *A family from Holland with much to share.*
La Chevaline, Fanjeaux, near Carcassonne.

"It's a real pleasure for us to have contact with our visitors" says Mr Van Dijk *"compared to our pretty lonely work in the vineyards from November to June. And to help them discover this region, as we discovered it seventeen years ago, when we came here from Holland, seduced by the variety of this landscape beneath the Mediterranean sun. We're always available, and we like to give the service that's given us our good reputation – we fetch fresh bread from the village every morning, look after the children if the parents want an evening out, make ice cubes in our freezer, lend books and board games, and sort out all sorts of problems, from a forgotten sleeping bag to a missing screw for a bike. Ours is a base for visiting all the treasures of the region – the plains of wheat and sunflowers, the vineyards, the foothills of the Pyrenees, the history, the Canal du Midi, Carcassonne, mediaeval Mirepoix and much more. It's also a calm place where you can relax – just a friendly little family business".*

☎ **04 68 24 75 33**

---

103 *Pocket of peace near Europe's biggest fortress.*
La Bastide de Madame, near Carcassonne.
The spot on which Monsieur and Madame Augé's site sits was popular with Stone Age hunters. The Augés haven't owned it for quite that long, but they have been camping and caravanning for years. Their site, they say, is run according to the great tradition of real camping – respect for the privacy of others and their right to tranquility. On the side of a hill, surrounded by interesting old farm buildings, it looks across the Corbiéres region to the Black Mountain and the Pyrenees. Right in the heart of the Cathar country, there's history and heritage to discover all around – ask the Augés, and

they'll help you plan an itinerary or two. Just up the road – five kilometres – is spectacular Carcassonne, the biggest fortress in Europe, inviolable for four hundred years till finally conquered by Simon de Montfort at the beginning of the thirteenth century. The size of a town, it has a hundred or so inhabitants, now permanently besieged by the hundreds of thousands of tourists who pour through its gates to see if it's really as magical as it looks from the road, or maybe just to see if it's real – it is, a fairytale castle on a grand scale, although neither Viollet-le-Duc's restoration nor the countless sellers of tacky souvenirs do much for its atmosphere. Back at the site, you'll find an altogether calmer atmosphere, where campers from all over the world can enjoy the peace of the countryside pretty much as their prehistoric predecessors did.

☎ **04 68 26 80 06 Fax 04 68 26 91 65**

104 In the lovely grounds of a famous abbey. Camping Val d'Aleth, Alet les Bains.

It took Christine and Christopher Cranmer two closely-typed pages to tell us everything about their fascinating site – which was once the gardens of the famous old abbey you can see in the picture. The wall which borders it is the old city wall (twelfth century). The little town in which all this sits is Alet-les-Bains, a beautifully-preserved mediaeval settlement now attracting visitors from all over the world. Camp here, in the serene, wooded abbey gardens, and you're two hundred metres from the boulangerie and the shops in one of the loveliest places in the South of France. The Cranmers, 'aided' by their two little daughters, have restored it all with loving care and scrupulous attention to the character of this very special setting, and now have thirty pitches to offer for rather special camping. Just to add to its charms, the site is bordered on the opposite side from the city wall by the river Aude, so that you can swim and fish (in waters regularly stocked with trout) from the site. Difficult to imagine wanting to leave this place, but if you do, you'll find yourself in spectacular scenery. Explorers with a taste for mysteries might like to wander down the road to Rennes-le-Chateau, where in the 1890's a previously-impoverished parish priest suddenly became fabulously rich as result of discovering something hidden in the pillars of the altar in his church. Hundreds of books on the nature of the find have since been written – a well-publicised theory (most famously in the book 'Holy Blood, Holy Grail') is that the priest discovered, via keys, clues and maps, that Christ was buried nearby. An intriguing business, which still draws thousands to the village each year.

☎ **04 68 69 90 40 (Phone and Fax)** •OPEN• ALL YEAR

105 Riverside site high in the Pyrenees. Camping Mas Gaillac, Bézac.

A site for explorers crossing the Pyrenees into Spain or Andorra, or for those simply wanting to explore the Ariège, a remote and little-known region that can very definitely be described as 'unspoilt'. Large chunks of it feel virtually untouched; many of the roads are narrow and wind round mountains for hours without making a great deal of progress. It is, though, a fascinating place for lovers of the remote and the dramatic; its heather-clad valleys and stone houses, set against their backdrop of great mountains, have a still beauty. Man has lived here since his earliest days, and all over the Pyrenees are caves bearing witness to those distant days; cave paintings, sculptures and carvings.

Our little farm camp site (ten pitches) is in a perfect spot on the banks of the river Ariège, which, as you can see from the picture, has a beach and is excellent for swimming and general splashing around; you can play volleyball, table tennis and the bafflingly-named 'baby-foot' – table football – here. Wonderful walks and cycle rides. Nearby Pamiers is sizeable (thirteen thousand inhabitants) and has shops, bars, restaurants, banks and the like. It owes its atypical name to Count Roger the Second, who after the Crusades set up a twinning arrangement with Apamée, in the Middle East, presumably with a view to instigating a rather more cordial exchange of views than had been the case until then. Walk round the Promenade du Castella (the old chateau walls, in French – the Spanish influence starts to leak across the border in these parts) and discover a bust of composer Fauré, of Requiem fame, who was born here.

☎ **05 61 67 14 54**

Foreign Fields

106 *A pleasant distraction near Macon and motorway.*

Ferme Equestre Malafretaz.

An interesting place to stop not far from Macon and not far from the motorway – this is a farm/riding stables, which also has six pitches for camping and a little auberge. Camp in a shady corner, and enjoy the peace and quiet. Admire the horses, and if you want to, ride them – there are mounts of every category here, from the high-speed high-jumping variety best left to the experts to friendly little ponies for the children to pet and play with. Beginners, says Corinne, need a horse which is sensible, calm and patient; she'll find one for you, and take you through the basics (getting on, staying on, getting off in a manner that makes it look as if you meant to). You can go out trekking for anything from a hour to a whole holiday. This is a cheery, friendly place, fun whether you take to horseback or simply enjoy camping on the farm; a huge bonus is the auberge restaurant, offering good country food and wine within staggering distance of the site (the Beaujolais area is just up the road, and it is, after all, only reasonable to support the local economy). As an alternative to four-legged travel, there's swimming, fishing and water-ski-ing on offer just two kilometres away. A site to distract you from the horrors of long hours on the motorway.

☎ **04 74 30 81 19 (phone & fax)** •OPEN• ALL YEAR

107 *Near the motorway and bucolic Bourg.*
Camping Le Potay, near Bourg-en-Bresse.

If you're sneaking over the border to Switzerland or simply meandering around the pretty countryside to the west of Geneva, then this little site just off the motorway near Bourg-en-Bresse could be a useful one. Monsieur Jacquet's farm is on the edge of a village with shops; he has seven pitches in a verdant and tranquil corner, with lovely leg-stretching walks all around and tennis and boules on site. There are spectacular drives around here; take the scenic road to the east and discover the valley and gorges of the river Ain. Go west and you'll find the busy and amiable town of Bourg-en-Bresse, a large but supremely rustic place which each year has a competition for the best dead chicken floating in milk. The 'unfortunate princess' Marguerite came from here; orphaned at the age of two, she was married at three to Charles, Dauphin of France, only to have the marriage annulled when her fiancé opted for the wealthy heir to Britanny instead. At seventeen she married the heir to the Spanish throne, who died a few months later. At twenty-one she married the Duke of Savoie, who caught a cold and died three years later. She gave up at this stage and devoted herself to running Holland and this part of France; she did it extremely well, and earned herself a special place in the affection of the people of Bourg. Enjoy this simple little farm site, and enjoy this honest country town too.

☎ **04 74 51 31 95**

108 *Looking across the lake to Switzerland. L'Ermitage des Clouz, near Evian-les-Bains.*

Amiable Monsieur Schmitt, proprietor of L'Ermitage des Clouz, is the holder of the Diplôme dEtat d'Accompagnateur en Montagne, which given the location of his site is not surprising. It's nine hundred metres up, on the Plateau de Gavot, overlooking Lake Léman (on the opposite shore of which are Geneva and Lausanne). You don't quite need skis and your own St Bernard to get there – as you can see, the slopes are gentle where the site is – but if you enjoy the exhilaration of mountain air and dramatic views you'll love this place, with its panoramic views and carefully-preserved, natural setting. It's quiet, calm and well organised, with barbecues, boules, croquet and a communal room containing tourist information, a library of books and board games. All sorts of strenuous activities on offer for those who like that sort of thing, from sailing on the lake to 'rafting and canoeing in torrents'. Those who don't will find the views, and the peace, supremely therapeutic – nearby health resorts like Evian-les-Bains have made their fortunes from being in this area. It's touring country par excellence; Monsieur Schmitt, who obviously thinks on a grand scale, recommends for excursions the village down the road, Switzerland and Italy.

☎ **04 50 73 60 66/04 50 70 26 22**

109 *Meadow overlooking the mountains. Le Trepu, Les Echelles, near Chambery.*

A six-pitch farm site on what's described as a 'vast meadow', which, as you can see from the photo, is no exaggeration – if you're longing to feel the grass instead of the accelerator pedal beneath your feet, this is for you. It's six hundred metres up in the fresh air, a long way from roads and overlooking the Massif de la Chartreuse, which is, as they say, massive, and the Grande Chartreuse, the massivest bit of the lot. Close by is a forest, a rambler's paradise, and two kilometres away you can fish in a trout stream. 'Les Echelles' is the nearest town, six kilometres of very scenic road away, with all facilities and a market on Tuesdays; Chambery is thirty kilometres away. You'll have to drive round several mountains to get there; remember when planning expeditions in this regions that all the roads except the main ones can be tricky. Don't even think about the little ones if you're driving a large vehicle or towing a caravan, if you're a nervous driver or if the weather's bad. When you get to Chambery, look for the Elephant Fountain, the cathedral and the chateau of the Dukes of Savoy. This is a busy commercial centre, with plenty of smart shops; you can get the train to Turin from here.

☎ **04 76 31 10 57**

Foreign Fields

110 **Farm on the edge of the Ardeche, minutes from the motorway.**
Monsieur Monteil, Flaviac, near Privas.
Leave the A7 'Autoroute du Soleil' after you've crossed the Drôme, take the N304 and cross the Rhône and before you know it you're in the Ardèche, where all the roads are green and squiggly and the scenery's out of this world. Leave the traffic behind and stop at this little farm site on the edge of it. There are six pitches, situated on the banks of a river; there are walks so wonderful you'll want to stay a week. You can shop and eat in the village, fish and buy farm produce, swim in a pool and play tennis nearby. Chances are that once you've discovered this corner you'll want to explore it further; if you're going south, take the road through Privas to Aubenas, then find the 'D' roads and follow the Ardèche valley through Vallon Pont-d'Arc, through the spectacular gorges and back onto the motorway via Pont-St Esprit. A little bit of old France before you join the new world again.

☎ **04 75 65 74 11**

111 **Meeting (and eating) the snails on a fruit farm.**
Les Marroniers, Montréal, Ardèche.
This is 'Les Marroniers', a fresh-food-lover's dream of a campsite on a fruit farm with its own auberge. *"At the foot of the mountain, on the edge of the river, in a Mediterranean climate, you'll find our little country site; it's quiet, and shaded by the chestnut trees and the cherry orchards"* says owner Sébastian. *'You'll have the farm all around you, with the fruit trees (peaches, apples, kiwi fruit, cherries), our plantation of Ginkgo Biloba, the soft fruits (strawberries and raspberries) and the vegetables. You can meet the farm animals, including sheep and snails, chickens and ducks. You'll find that our Ardèche is a region of enormously varied landscapes, whether you go out by car, by horse or on foot, or even by canoe down the river. It's also a place of culture, with its rich heritage of the past".* When you've finished saying hello to the snails and working out what a Ginkgo Biloba is, we suggest you explore the dining room of the auberge restaurant (where if you wish you can EAT the snails, among many other delightful-sounding delicacies). And for a little snack to take back to your quarters you might pop into the farm shop, where, depending on the season, they have cherries, strawberries, raspberries, melons, peaches, plums, courguettes, potatoes, lettuce, tomatoes, eggs, fruit juice, jam ....

☎ **04 75 36 82 54 (phone and fax)**

112 At the foot of the cliffs by the Ardèche river.
La Falaise, Balazuc.

'La Falaise' means 'the cliff', and as you can see this little site couldn't really be called anything else. It's by the side of the Ardéche river, in a lovely valley lined with orchards, and this great outcrop of chalky rock provides a dramatic backdrop (in keeping with the spirit of the region, which is FULL of dramatic backdrops). Monsieur and Madame Berre, who run this happy little place, think the calm and beauty of it all are wonderful, and so do their visitors. The small building in the picture is multi-talented, providing a reception office, a snack bar and a meeting-room for campers – what, alas, the photo doesn't show you is the great expanse of green, well-shaded land by the edge of the river where you can play volleyball, experiment with boules or just simply relax. Seasoned explorers will recognise a place to abscond to with a good book when they see one. If you wish you can hire a canoe and career down the river; alternatively you can walk for miles along this beautiful valley. The village of Balazuc, with shops and a restaurant, is but a lazy stroll away. The famous Ardèche gorges, with all their cliffs, caves and spectacular hairpin bends, are no distance as the crow flies but quite a way as the road wiggles – these are wiggles worth following, though. Astonishingly, you're no distance here from the A7 'Route du Soleil' motorway. An excellent site where a quick stopover could last days.

☎ **04 75 37 74 27**

---

113 Peaceful pine forest in nougat country.
Monsieur Gilles, Roynac, near Montélimar.

There is no great shortage of space at Monsieur Gilles' site – he has thirty two acres of land and six pitches. Camp in the shade of the trees on the edge of a vast pine forest and enjoy the outlook, the peace and the scent of the pines. If you've been travelling on the motorway (and enjoying the outlook of the back of the lorry in front, the less-than-peaceful roar of turbo-charged Renaults in the outside lane and the smell of exhaust fumes) you'll be delighted to know that this little haven of tranquillity is just a short plunge into the countryside away. If you haven't done it before, take time to explore the nice old city of Montélimar, famous for its nougat. Train travellers will know that when the Paris train stops

here an army of nougat vendors besiege it and tempt passengers with their wares, conducting their business at breakneck speed and jumping off the train again just as it starts moving; Henry James had the same experience when he took his 'little tour' nearly a century ago. Consider, from here, taking the little roads across country and slipping into glorious Provence by its equally glorious back door, the lovely land surrounding lofty Mont Ventoux.

☎ **04 75 90 11 18 (phone and fax)**

114 *On a farm where sparkling wine is made.*

Monsieur Roury, Pontaix, near Die.
Monsieur Roury is a vineyard proprietor, and the grapes he grows on his farm in the valley go on to become 'Clairette de Die', a lovely sparkling wine. You can camp on his farm – he's got ten pitches – and see for yourself how it's done. You can buy his wine too; it's a real pleasure, on some dark winter day, to open a bottle and remember the place from which it came. The farm is close to the village of Pontaix, which sits right on the edge of the river which gives its name to the region. It's big enough for shopping and eating out, and if you're feeling energetic you can scramble up the hill to the top, where there are both ruins and a view to admire. Close by is the town of Die, packed with little shops and cafés, which gives its name to Monsieur Roury's wine. It was founded by the Romans as a fortress town. Sad to think that two thousand years later this beautiful area was still the scene of military activity; in the Second World War the Resistance movement was very active in these parts, whole villages were destroyed and many lives were lost. Enjoy the peace of it all now, though – this is a place which has all the prettiness and charm of Provence plus a hint of the flavour of the Alps.

☎ **04 75 21 22 14**

115 *Auberge camping in the land of lime-blossom and lavender.*

Le Moulin de Cost, Buis-les-Baronnies.
This is the garden of the auberge at the 'Moulin de Cost', where you sit outside late into the warm Provençal evening and enjoy traditional country cooking at its best.
Choose trout or crayfish fresh from the tank, or opt for some of the proprietor's home made sausages, paté and smoked meats. Eating inside, in the whitewashed vaulted cellars of this handsome old building is a real pleasure too. The auberge has thirty pitches for camping in a quiet corner down by the river, where you can swim and fish. Fresh bread is delivered every morning,

and there are all sorts of treats to buy – wine, goats' cheese, poultry, eggs, honey, jams and the famous charcuterie. Splash about in the pool as much as you like, wander round the farm or meander into the village of Buis-les-Baronnies, which describes itself simply as 'a fragment of Paradise'. It's an area famed for its climate (no rain, little wind, plenty of sun and blue sky, cool nights), its lime blossom and its lavender – the perfume of Provence. Mountains, sometimes snow-capped, provide drama on the horizon, but here the altitude is modest (500 metres), making it perfect rambling and pony-trekking country. Explorers with a passion for more exalted altitudes can climb Mont Ventoux (1,909 metres), where the temperature at the top is eleven degrees centigrade lower than that at the bottom, and where the Mistral blows furiously. You can drive to the top; the world record time for doing it is nine minutes, at an average speed of 142 kilometres per hour.

☎ **04 75 28 09 82 Fax 04 75 28 08 23**

116 *Hang-gliding, camping and country cooking.*

Auberge de Monteglin, Laragne.

A launch pad and landing ground for hang-gliders (together with a shuttle service to take you there) are among the less-conventional-than-usual features on offer at this farm-auberge camp site. Explore the air currents if you will, or simply sit and watch outside the auberge if you'd rather keep your feet on the ground. Fifty pitches for camping here, so not a tiny site, but certainly one with a difference; there's plenty of room, and you can choose to be in the orchard or in the meadow. Look hard at the photo and you'll catch a glimpse of the mountain scenery behind the buildings. This is a stunning setting, in a lovely climate, where the skies, say proprietor Monsieur Trupheme, are the colours of gold and lavender. The auberge serves excellent meals at sixty-nine francs, and breakfasts at twenty, and there's farm produce to buy and a town (Laragne) nearby for serious provisioning. No end of activities are on offer, mostly of the hardy variety – there are trips on various rivers by raft and canoe, hikes, mountain bike excursions and a whole range of airborne possibilities. You could take a gentler approach, though, and explore the spectacular nearby lakes, gorges and mountain villages in more conventional style. A lot of fun, this site.

☎ 04 92 65 02 94 **Fax 04 92 65 00 76**   •OPEN• ALL YEAR

117 *Still waters and raging torrents.*

Belle-Vue, Crillon-le-Brave, Vaucluse.

Twenty-five pitches here, with a pretty pool and a stupendous view. This is the Vaucluse plateau, a typically Provençal landscape of lavender (when the little round bushes are cropped it looks for all the world as if the fields are planted with hedgehogs) with great goings-on underground. The rock soaks up the rain as soon as it lands and sucks it down into a subterranean world of caves, potholes, stalactites, stalagmites and tunnels. A great deal of it comes thundering out of the rock again in spectacular style at the Fountain of Vaucluse. Worth some serious exploration to find this place, ideally in spring or in winter when the emerald-green torrent is at its most dramatic, foaming and vapourising on the rocks. Less drama at this little site, but a friendly welcome from Monsieur and Madame Masclaux, local wine and farm produce to buy and some excellent walking and cycling routes (and the picturesque village of Crillon-le-Brave) nearby. A trip into nearby Carpentras is worthwhile; it's been there since the Celts, its fortunes rising and falling regularly ever since. In the eighteenth century irrigation works transformed the barren plain into fertile land, creating a thriving agricultural base which still supports the town today.

☎ 04 90 62 42 29 **Fax 04 90 62 34 55**

Foreign Fields

118 *Near fruity Apt in the colourful Luberon.*

Les Jonquiers, St Martin de Castillon.

This is the Saturday market in Apt, capital of the intoxicating Luberon area of Provence, jellied fruit sweet centre of the universe. Everywhere you look in this delightful, bustling little town you'll find box upon box of the sugary, fruity delicacies – the raw materials flourish and ripen easily here under the Provençal sun. In Apt also is refined the raw ochre which gives its golden-red colour to so much of the surrounding countryside. You can follow the fifty-kilometre 'Ochre Trail' through Pont Julien, Roussillon (gory legend, spectacular cliffs, best contemplated from an excellent restaurant whose tables overlook them), St Saturnin and finally Colorado, a name which explains itself when you get there. Monsieur and Madame Mangeot run a lovely little site nearby, with a truly magnificent view over the Grand Luberon mountains. They have twenty-five pitches on an airy, south-facing plateau, with plenty of trees for shade and an atmosphere of tranquillity and order. Drink pure water from the spring, and wander in the lavender fields and woods surrounding it all. The Mangeots organise rambles from the site across this lovely countryside to see its natural wonders – they're very knowledgeable, and their running commentary brings to life the things you're seeing. If you want to go further, you have all the most beautiful places in Provence within eighty kilometres – Monsieur Mangeot thought of thirty-six without really trying. Games on the site, and a village close by – one of those corners where you'll simply want to stay.

☎ **04 90 75 20 11 fax 04 90 75 25 49/04 90 75 12 44**

119 *Provençal farm in lavender-distilling hamlet.*

Camping des Mouguets, Castellet, near Apt.

Camp in the grounds of the farmhouse you can see right in the centre of this picture of the lovely Luberon, just to the south of Apt. Close by is the hamlet of Castellet, which has seventy or eighty inhabitants and two lavender distilleries, where the precious oil is extracted from the flowers and processed ready for the perfume industry. The harvest (increasingly mechanised) is in July and August. Look out for the upstart 'lavandin', a plant of superior yield but inferior quality used for the perfuming of cleaning materials and the like, now representing a third of the acreage of the Provence 'lavender' fields. Lots of pretty, quiet roads here, ideal for cycling (see photo again), and wonderful walks and car tours round picture-book villages set in lovely landscapes. Back at the site there's everything you need for comfortable camping, and produce to buy; major refuelling is best done in Apt, where there are supermarkets and lots of little food shops. Uncomplicated, classic farm camping (ten pitches) in the very heart of Provence.

☎ **04 90 75 28 62** *OPEN ALL YEAR*

120 In the land of the potters and the Grand Canyon.

Ferme de Vauvenieres, Saint Jurs, near Moustiers-Ste-Marie.

This is the Ferme de Vauvenieres, surrounded by lavender fields and sheltered by mountains, about as typical of Alpes de Haute Provence as you can get! There's a warm welcome here from Héléne and Christian Sauvaire, who have a camp site with twenty-five pitches on the farm – there are boules, volley ball and a little play-hut with games for children. They're on the edge of Saint Jurs – "a little village clinging to the mountain of Mondenier which has known how to preserve its traditional character, both in its architecture and in its welcome". From its vantage point nine hundred metres up, there's Provence as far as the eye can see; it has a little café-restaurant, two potters and in summer three times the population as all its holiday-home owners flock back to the south. Explore nearby Moustiers-Ste-Marie, famous for its painted ceramics, usually in the brilliant blues and yellows that are so typically Provence; potters, and pots to buy, abound here, as do good restaurants. High above the village is a 700-feet long chain strung between the tops of two mountains by a returning Crusader glad to be home. And whatever else you explore in Provence, don't miss the Grand Canyon du Verdon. Completely ignored by the locals, who would rather have had good farming land there instead, till this century, it's now a major tourist attraction, genuinely as dramatic as (if smaller than) its American namesake.

☎ **04 92 74 44 18 (phone and fax)**

121 Grapes and olives, Greeks and Romans.
Vignobles des Hautes Collines de la Cote d'Azur, near Vence.

Monsieur Rasse lives close to Cannes, Nice and Monte Carlo, very trendy places, but he's not too concerned about all that. On his farm, he tends vines and olive trees and ponders on who planted the first ones there – was it the Greeks, or the Romans? He points out that olives have been pressed, and wine poured into amphora, on this site for thousands of years, and that the landscape has been shaped by countless generations of people doing just what he's doing now. Come and camp here, and see it all for yourself, under the hot sun and brilliant blue skies of Provence Maritime. Quite a few pitches (seventy-five) but lots of space, and a rare haven of rural tranquillity close to the French Riviera. Which has, of course, to be explored: Nice is nice (though Grahame Greene didn't think so); the old town is certainly worth a visit, and the food's good. Cannes in very much a matter of taste, which is less evident than money in this glitzy place. The whole coast is spectacularly beautiful, which is why these haunts of the rich and famous came to be here in the first place. Monsieur Rasse is neither rich nor famous, but he's extremely happy with his little patch of Provence beneath him and his two thousand years of heritage behind him. He's close to the village, Saint-Jeannet, and the town of Vence, which has a market every day in the old Roman forum, and a chapel built and decorated by Matisse as a thank-you to the nuns who nursed him through a serious illness here.

☎ **04 93 24 96 01 (phone and fax)**

Foreign Fields

122 *An almond farm between the Alpilles and the Camargue.*
Les Amandaies, Mouries.

A gloriously peaceful little site on a farm which grows almonds, right at the foot of the Rhône valley. Just six pitches, surrounded by meadows of hay, miles from the madding crowds but close to the main roads and motorways for exploring Provence to the East and the Languedoc to the west. You may not bother, though, when you discover the Alpilles, right behind you, a tiny patch of very distinctive terrain, craggy white rocks, caves and dark vegetation, olive trees, almond trees and pines. Seek out the imposing ruined Aqueducts de Barbegal, and explore dramatic Baux, perched on its strange plateau. The lords of Baux were a troublesome bunch; claiming descent from one of the Biblical 'three kings', they ran amok causing civil war and mayhem for centuries. Take yourself off to the Camargue, marshland populated by wild horses, flamingos, birds and little black bulls, and explore it by bike if you possibly can – the best bits are off the main car routes. Follow Henry James to Roman Arles, about which he was a little confused, although finally he declared it charming, as do most people. Stock up on the wonderful food and inexpensive wine of the region, then take yourself back to Monsieur and Madame Crouau's farm. They've got a barbecue there; light it, find something to cook and sit in the shade of the almond trees admiring the views over the meadows and the hills. A little corner well worth knowing about.

☎ **04 90 47 50 59 Fax 04 90 47 61 79**

STOP PRESS • STOP PRESS • STOP PRESS

Five super little sites which slipped in at the last moment –
full details in the Reference Section at the back in the usual way.

123 Le Cator, Simorre (Gers).

Six-pitch farm site in beautiful valley ..... D'Artagnan country, in the deep south! ..... Gascon cuisine ..... excellent walks/cycling..... historical sites nearby ..... open all year ..... multi-lingual proprietor!

☎ 05 62 65 33 44 Fax 05 62 65 30 99

124 Monsieur and Madame Jarry, La Croixille (Mayenne).

Peaceful farm site far from noisy roads ..... pretty touring country ..... six pitches ..... organised walks ..... bike outings ..... slide shows ..... Normandy/Britanny borders ..... amiable owners!

☎ 02 43 68 57 00

125 Camping Le Ronquet, Agon-Coutainville (Manche).

One kilometre from the sea on Gulf of St Malo (Normandy) ..... lovely Cotentin peninsular ..... twenty-five pitches ..... cycle routes ..... horseriding nearby.

☎ 02 33 47 05 29

126 Camping Le Jardin, Vezins (Manche).

Close to Mont St Michel, Normandy ..... twelve pitches (orchard/meadow) ..... friendly (English) owners ..... open all year ..... children's games/entertainment ..... near Normandy battlefields ..... excellent walks.

☎ 02 33 48 25 83

127 Camping La Roquette (Var).

Near St Tropez..... sea fifteen kilometres..... just off motorway..... on banks of river..... close to shops..... excellent rock climbing..... fishing..... barbecues.

☎ 04 94 45 78 61 (Phone and Fax)

Foreign Fields

Reference Section Northern France

In this section you will find the essential information you need for contacting and finding sites, together with a listing of the site's facilities, charges, periods of opening and nearby amenities.

Prices quoted are normally for a caravan or motor caravan pitch for two persons for one night excluding any supplementary charges for electric hook-ups, awnings, additional persons, etc. For further information please contact the site directly.

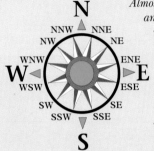

Almost all sites in France provide the basic facilities of drinking water and a disposal point for chemical waste. Most also have toilets and washing facilities/showers (abbreviated here as 'shwrs').

To help you find sites readily on the map, each set of directions begins with the approximate distance and compass direction of the site from a major city or town. Distances are measured in kilometres 'as the crow flies' (i.e., in a straight line) from the centre of the city, normally its cathedral. Sixteen points of the compass are used to give the direction.

Northern France

1. **Camping a la Ferme**, Rue des Champs, 62310 Verchin. M. MACQUET. Tel 03 21 41 64 87. 12 pitches. 50F. Apr-Sept. 55km SE of Calais; 27km S of St Omer. From St Omer follow D928 to Fruges, then L via D93 to Verchin. Site is on D93 4km from Verchin.
On site/nearby: toilets, shwrs, elec hook-ups, laundry facilities, payphone, shop, meals.

2. **Camping a la Ferme**, 8 La Neuve Rue, 60480 Oursel-Maison. Sebastien & Odile FONTANA. Tel 03 44 46 81 55. 6 Pitches. 45F incl electricity. All year. 18km NNE of Beauvais. From Beauvais, take N1 to Froissy, then L onto D151. After 7km R to Francastel. Site is between Francastel and Oursel-Maison on D10.
On site/nearby: toilets, shwrs, elec hook-ups, payphone.

North East France

3. **Le Terne Jean Servais**, 08380 Brognon. M. & Mme ALAVOINE-COLINET. Tel 03 24 53 50 27. 25 pitches. 37F. mid Apr-mid Oct.
35km WNW of Charleville-Mezieres via N43, before Hirson. Turn R for Brognon via Signy-le-Petit.
On site/nearby: toilets, shwrs, elec hook-ups, laundry facilities, payphone, shop, meals.

4. **Le Faucon**, 08800 Nohan-sur-Semoy, Thilay. Jean Paul PERESSON. Tel 03 24 41 26 78 Fax 03 24 41 75 58. 25 pitches. 45F. Mid June-Aug.15km NNE of Charleville-Meziers. On D31 between Montherme and Les Hautes Rivieres, on bank of River Semoy.
On site/nearby: toilets, shwrs, payphone, meals.

5. **Le Moulin d'en Haut**, 10 Rue de Moulin, 77139 Etrepilly. M. VION. Tel 01 64 36 61 34. 20 pitches. 45F. Mid Apr-mid Oct. 10km N of Meaux (40km E of Paris) via D405; turn L for Etripilly after 7km. From Autoroute A1, exit at Senlis, go twds Meaux. In Saint Soupplets, at lights, L twds Chateau Thierry for 9 km. In Etrepilly, Rue du Moulin is on R, 100m before church.
On site/nearby: toilets, shwrs, elec hook-ups, payphone, shop.

6. **Ferme de la Croix Villiere**, Neuville-Day, 08130 Attigny. Annick & Remi COUTEL. Tel 03 24 71 44 19 fax 03 24 71 68 15. 12 pitches. All year. 54km NE of Reims between Attigny and le Chesne off D25. Day is 1km N of Neuville.
On site/nearby: toilets, shwrs, elec hook-ups, laundry facilities, payphone, rstrnt.

7. **13 Rue de l'Evangile**, 51300 Luxemont. Anne SCHERSCHELL. Tel 03 26 74 09 57. 40F. Apr-Sept. 34km SE of Chalons-s-Marne, and 5km SE of Vitry-le-Francais on D316 by Canal de la Marne.
On site/nearby: toilets, shwrs, elec hook-ups, payphone.

8. **Camping Hautoreille**, 52630 Bannes. Elisabeth STORZ & Mani BENSINGER. Tel 03 25 84 83 40. 100 pitches. 40F. Closed Oct. 60km NNE of Dijon, 6km NW of Langres on D74 just before Bannes.
On site/nearby: toilets, shwrs, elec hook-ups, laundry facilities, payphone, shop, rstrnt.

9. La Renaudine, 70800 Dampierre les Conflans. Claudine THEVENOT. Tel 03 84 49 82 34. 6 pitches. 40F. 24km N of Vesoul. From Vesoul take D10 in dirctn of St Loup. After Conflans-s-Lanterne L onto D45 for 4km.
On site/nearby: toilets, shwrs, elec hook-ups, payphone, shop, meals.

10 . Camping a la Ferme, route de Belleherbe, 25380 Charmoille. Renee & Claude MONNIN. Tel 03 81 44 30 29. 15 pitches. 54F. May-Sept. 48km E of Besancon, via D32, 11 km W of Maiche; Charmoille is 2km S of Belleherbe.
On site/nearby: toilets, shwrs, elec hook-ups, laundry facilities.

Central France

11. La Ferme des Hautes Frenes, 10130 Eaux-Puiseaux. Marie-Paule & Francis LAMBERT. Tel 03 25 42 15 04 fax 03 25 42 02 95. 6 pitches. 50F incl electricity. All year. 24km SSW of Troyes twds Auxerres by RN77; turn R onto CD111 twds Eaux-Puiseaux. Follow signs to Camping a la Ferme.
On site/nearby: toilets, shwrs, elec hook-ups, laundry facilities, payphone, shop, rstrnt.

12. Au Relax Vert, Les Bourgoins, 89520 Saints-en Puisaye, Bourgogne. Huguette & Marcel MORIN. Tel 03 86 45 53 83; fax 03 86 45 59 33. 25 pitches. 38F. Mar-Oct. 28km SW of Auxerre. Take D965 to Toucy then D955 twds St Sauveur. After 9km L onto D211. Signed in 4km.
On site/nearby: toilets, shwrs, elec hook-ups, payphone, shop, rstrnt.

13. Camping a la Ferme, Les Chatelaines, 89200 Avallon. Gilles COIGNOT. Tel 03 86 34 16 37 fax 03 86 34 55 95. 24 pitches. 34F. All year. 43km SE of Auxerre. Site is 3km to S of Avallon in direction 'Vallee du Cousin' on D127 twds Usy & Domecy-s-Cure.
On site/nearby: toilets, shwrs, elec hook-ups, laundry facilities, payphone, shop, rstrnt.

14. Saute Mouton, La Reserve, 58340 Diennes-Aubigny. M. & Mme RYAN. Tel 03 86 50 04 34; fax 03 86 50 59 24. 6 pitches. 40F. All year. 30km SE of Nevers. From Nevers take D978 twds Chatillon-en-Bazois. R just before Rouy onto D34 twds La Machine and Decize. Continue to Anlezy then Ville-Langry. Then L onto D26 twds Cercy-la-Tour for 6.5km until you see Diennes-Aubigny signed on L.
On site/nearby: payphone, meals.

15. Camping a la Ferme, Monclain, 58800 La Collancelle. M. GOGUELAT B. Tel 03 86 22 41 89. 6 pitches. 30F. Easter-Oct. 41km NE of Nevers. On D958 halfway between Corbigny and St Saulge.
On site/nearby: toilets, shwrs, elec hook-ups.

16. Ferme de Prunay, 4150 Commune Seillac. Michel FOUCHAULT. Tel 02 54 70 02 01. Fax 02 54 70 11 53. Reservations 06 08 42 17 56. 25 pitches. 40F. Easter-Nov. 13km WSW of Blois. From Blois take N766 twds Angers & Chateau Renault as far as Molineuf, then L twds Seillac.
On site/nearby: toilets, shwrs, elec hook-ups, shop, rstrnt.

17. Camping de la Charmoise a Sassay, 41700 Loir et Cher. Christian FOINARD. Tel 02 54 79 55 15. 20 pitches. 24F. Easter-Oct. 24km SSE of Blois. Take D956 through Contres, then R after 3km to Sassay.
On site/nearby: toilets, shwrs, elec hook-ups, payphone.

18. La Belle Etoile, 41360 Lunay. Huguette & Robert ABLANCOURT. Tel 02 54 72 00 89. 6 pitches. 25F. All year. 11km W of Vendome. Take D5 twds Savigny-s-Bray. Lunay is off to the L after 7km.
On site/nearby: toilets, laundry facilities, payphone, shop, rstrnt.

19. La Huchette, 18410 Argent-sur-Sauldre. Jacqueline & Jack HUET. Tel 02 48 73 32 61. 30 Pitches. 39F. Apr-Sept. 52km SE of Orleans; 20km SW of Gien. From Gien take D940 to Argent sur Sauldre. Just before A-s-S turn R onto D176 for 3km.
On site/nearby: toilets, shwrs, elec hook-ups, payphone, shop, rstrnt.

20. Ferme Auberge St Malo, Champlieu, 71240 Etrigny. Jacqueline GOUJON. Tel 03 85 92 21 47/03 85 92 20 63 fax 03 85 92 22 13. 25 pitches. 39F. May-Oct. 10km from Tournus. From Tournus follow D215 twds St Gengoux-le-National. After 9km R at Nogent twds Nanton & Sennecy-le-Grand. After 3km L to Champlieu.
On site/nearby: toilets, shwrs, elec hook-ups, laundry facilities, payphone, meals.

21. Chez Gros Jean, 87160 St-Sulpice-les-Feuilles. Mr & Mrs Hartley SCOTT. Tel/fax 05 55 76 67 89. 5 pitches. 40F. All year. 55km N of Limoges. Leave Autoroute N20 at Exit 5. Follow signs to St-Sulpice-les-Feuilles, D912. Go thr' town. At Xrds with Gamm Vert Garden Centre on L, turn R & follow signs to 'Lavaupot & Chez Gros Jean'. Go thr' Lavauport; Chez Gros Jean is 0.5km further on.
On site/nearby: shop, rstrnt.

Foreign Fields

22. Les Quatre Vents, Mazand, Bessines-sur-Gartempe, 87250 Haut Vienee. Mrs June PICKERING.
Tel 05 55 76 37 26. 6 pitches. 50F. All year.
33km N of Limoges, off Autoroute N20, 4km from Bessines-s-G in valley of Gartempe river.
On site/nearby: toilet, shwr, elec hook-ups, laundry facilities, payphone, shop, rstrnt.

23. Les Vigeres, 87500 Le Chalard. Robert & Shirley DRURY. Tel 05 55 09 37 22; fax 05 55 09 93 39. 45 pitches.
All year. 32km SSW of Limoges. Follow D704 to St.Yrieux-la-Perche where turn R ont D901. Les Vigeres is 9km,
just past Le Chalard.
On site/nearby: toilets, shwrs, elec hook-ups, meals.

24. Le Petit Chaumeix, 23600 Malleret-Boussac. M. LADET Michel. Tel 05 55 65 06 46. 8 pitches. 32F. May-Sept. 34km
W of Montlucon. Take D916 to Boussac, then D15 for 6km to Malleret-B, which is on L.
On site/nearby: toilets, shwrs, elec hook-ups, laundry facilities, payphone, shop, rstrnt.

25. Abbaye de Prebenoit, 23270 Betete. Alain GERRANDON. Tel 05 55 80 78 91/05 55 83 80 95 fax 05 55 67 74 28.
Apr-Oct. 42km W of Montlucon; 23km NE of Gueret. From Gueret take D940 N to Genouillac, where turn R for
the Abbaye which is 2km E of Betete & 5 km N of Chatelus-Malvaleix.
On site/nearby: toilets, shwrs, elec hook-ups, laundry facilities, payphone, shop, rstrnt.

26. Camping a la Ferme, La Loge, 42220 Thelis-la-Combe. M. J. Michel GRANJON. Tel 04 77 39 65 25. 20 pitches.
30F. May-Oct. 19km SE of St Etienne. Take N82. Abt 5km before Bourg-Argental, turn L onto D29 twds Thelis-la-
C for abt 3km. Turn L at sign 'La Loge'.
On site/nearby: toilets, shwrs, elec hook-ups, laundry facilities, payphone, shop, rstrnt.

27. Chateau de la Grange Fort, Les Pradeaux, 63500 Issoire. Tel 04 73 71 05 93/04 73 71 02 43; fax 04 73 71 07 69.
Room for 125 tents & caravans. 34km SSE of Clermont-Ferrand. On A75 to S of Clermont-F take exit 13 at Issoire.
Take D996 to Parentignat, where go R (D999) for 200m. Then R onto D34 twds Pradeaux, where site is signed.
On site/nearby: toilets, shwrs, rstrnt.

28. Camping a la Ferme, Arsac, 19200 Confolent-Port-Dieu. Jean Louis LOURADOUR. Tel 05 55 94 50 52. 25 pitches.
25F. 50km SW of Clermont-Ferrand. From N89 between Bourg-Lastic and Ussel take D27 S to Confolent-P-D.
On site/nearby: toilets, shwrs, elec hook-ups.

29. La Pastourelle, Ruynes-en-Margeride, 15320 Lorcieres. M. Raymond MOUILLIER. Tel 04 71 23 40 68. 30F.
July-Sept. 90km S of Clermond-Ferrand; 12km ESE of St Flour. From Autoroute A75 exit 30. Ruynes-en-M is
12km by D50.
On site/nearby: toilets, shwrs, elec hook-ups, laundry facilities.

30. Camping de l'Etang, Merigot, 15270 Champs-sur-Tarentaine. M. & Mme Jean GERARD. Tel 04 71 78 71 36. 25
pitches. 37F. Apr-Oct. 55km SW of Clermont-Ferrand; 10km E of Bort-les-Orgues. From Bort-les-O take D679 to
Champs-sur-T, then take 'route des lacs' twds Marchal & Besse-en-Chandesse for 5km. On the plateau, take 2nd R.
On site/nearby: toilets, shwrs, elec hook-ups, laundry facilities, payphone, shop, rstrnt.

31. Acceuil a la Campagne, Route Imperiale, 43450 Espalem. Marinette et Clement DELAIR. Tel 04 71 76 20 50. 6
pitches. 42.50F. Apr-Oct. 60km S of Clermont-Ferrand; 4km from exit 22 of Autoroute A75. From this exit, take
direction W, D586, then D20. At Xrds with D653 take this road for 1km in S direction.
On site/nearby: toilets, shwrs, elec hook-ups, shop, rstrnt.

32. Les Marodons, 63290 Noalhat. M. & Mme Alain LE HALPER. Tel 04 73 94 10 30. 10 pitches. All year. 32km
NE of Clermont-Ferrand. On D906 between Thiers and Puy-Guillaume turn E onto D448 for Noalhat.
On site/nearby: toilets, shwrs, elec hook-ups, laundry facilities, payphone, shop, rstrnt.

North West France

33. Camping a la Ferme, La Moriniere, 50770 Pirou. M Claude MASSU. Tel 02 33 45 29 29; fax 02 33 45 88 26. 25
pitches. 55-60F. Easter-mid Sept. 53km S of Cherbourg. Off D650 to E, S of Lessay, 2km S of village of Pirou.
On site/nearby: toilets, shwrs, elec hook-ups, laundry facilities, payphone.

34. Camping Le Puits, La Groudiere, 14350 St Martin-des-Besaces. Barbara & Barry ASHWORTH & family. Tel/fax 02
31 67 80 02. 25 pitches. 60F. Feb-Nov. 41km SW of Caen. On RN175 Caen-Avranches road, 12km from Villers-Bocage.
On site/nearby: toilets, shwrs, elec hook-ups, laundry facilities, payphone, shop, rstrnt.

35. Le Carreau, 76970 Flamanville. Serge & Brigitte QUEVILLY. Tel 02 35 96 85 57. 25 pitches. 40F. Mid Mar-mid
Nov. 30km NW of Rouen. 2km to E of junction of N15 and N29 by Yvetot.
On site/nearby: toilets, shwrs, elec hook-ups, payphone, shop, meals, rstrnt.

36. Le Goulet, 76680 St Saens. Mme Monique GOUTCHOT. Tel/fax 02 35 34 51 26. 8 pitches. 21F. All year. 29km NNE of Rouen. Off Autoroute A28 between exits 10 & 11.
On site/nearby: toilets.

37. Camping a la Ferme, La Febvrerie, 27260 St Sylvestre-de-Cormeilles. Mme Claire MARAIS. Tel 02 32 42 29 69. 25 pitches. 29F. All year. 57km E of Caen; 18km NE of Lisieux. 3km off D27 to E.
On site/nearby: toilets, shwrs, elec hook-ups.

38. Les Marroniers, 27680 Ste Opportune-la-Mare (Hamlet of Buquetterie). M. Jean GUILLIET. Tel 02 32 42 14 52. 25 pitches. 45F. Apr-Oct.
42km W of Rouen. Autoroute A13, exit Bourneville. L twds Ste Opportune-la-M. Follow signs.
On site/nearby: toilets, shwrs, elec hook-ups, payphone, rstrnt.

39. Camping a la Ferme Monsallier, St Croix-sur-Orne, (Route Lac de Rabodanges), 61210 Putanges-Pont-Ecrepin. M. MONSALLIER. Tel 02 33 35 05 98 fax 02 33 36 67 45. 12 pitches. 36F. Mid June-mid Sept. 43km S of Caen; 15km SSE of Falaise. From Falaise take D909 S. Turn R at Bazoche-au-Houlme onto D121 to Lac de Rabodanges.
On site/nearby: toilets, shwrs, elec hook-ups, payphone, rstrnt.

40. La Gargouillere, 53600 Mezangers. M. & Mme Georges NAVEAU. Tel 02 43 90 65 12. 6 pitches. 28F. Apr-Oct. 28km NE of Laval. 5km NW of Evron on D7.
On site/nearby: toilets, shwrs, elec hook-ups, laundry facilities, rstrnt.

41. La Noe, 61600 Lonlay Le Tesson. Alan & Linda FIRKINS. Tel 02 33 37 27 71. 6 pitches. 80F. 60km S of Caen. On D924 Between Argentan and Flers, take D20 S through Briouze for 7km.
On site/nearby: elec hook-ups, laundry facilities, payphone, shop.

42. Le Plessis, 72510 Mansigne. M. Maxime BOUSSARD. Tel 02 43 46 10 81. 6 pitches. 20F. Mid June-Oct. 30km S of Le Mans. Take N23 SW from Le Mans as far as Cerans-Fouiletourte. Fork L at lights twds Oize, where take D31 to Mansigne. At the village take the shore road; 2nd farm on left.
On site/nearby: toilets, shwrs, elec hook-ups, shop, rstrnt.

Western France

43. Camping a la Ferme de Croas-Men, 29610 Plouigneau. M. & Mme Danial COTTY. Tel 02 98 79 11 50. 25 pitches. 50F. Mid Apr-mid Nov.
7km E of Morlaix; 4km NW of Plouigneau just to E of Garlan, from where it is signed.
On site/nearby: toilets, shwrs, elec hook-ups, laundry facilities, payphone, shop, rstrnt.

44. Saint Clair, Plonevez-du-Faou, 29530 Finistere. David & Mary Archer. Tel/fax 02 98 73 94 45. 70F. All year. 36km S of Morlaix on D36 3km S of Loqueffret.
On site/nearby: toilets, shwrs, elec hook-ups, payphone, shop, rstrnt.

45. Camping a la Ferme, Logan, Pouldreuzic, 29710. M. & Mme Jean & Bernadette GUINLE. Tel 02 98 54 41 14. 25 pitches. 65F. 19km WSW of Quimper. From Pouldreuzic go N twds Douarnenez for 1.5km and turn L for site.
On site/nearby: toilets, shwrs, elec hook-ups, laundry facilities, payphone, shop, rstrnt.

46. Camping Les Genets d'Or, Kermerour, Pont Kereon , 29380 Bannalec, South Finistere. Alan & Judy THOMAS. Tel/fax 02 98 39 54 35. 50F. Apr-Oct. 31km ESE of Quimper; 1km from Bannalec.
On site/nearby: toilets, shwrs, elec hook-ups, payphone, shop, rstrnt.

47. Feuntinigou, Botcanou, Glomel, 22110 Rostrenen. Sybil BLACKBURN. Tel/fax 02 96 29 12 34. 6 pitches. All year. 56km SW of St Brieuc. From Rostrenen take D790 twds Plouray for 6km.
On site/nearby: toilets, shwrs, elec hook-ups, payphone, shop, rstrnt.

48. Coat Boloi, 22740 Pleudaniel. Keith STADDON. Tel 02 96 20 16 59. 8 pitches. 30F. Apr-Oct. 22km N of Guincamp. On D787 between Pontriuex and Lezardrieux.
On site/nearby: toilets, shwrs, elec hook-ups, payphone, shop, rstrnt.

49. Manoir de la Villeneuve, St Aaron, 22400 Lamballe. M. de CUVERVILLE. Tel 02 96 31 01 71. 25 pitches. 50F. Mid June-mid Sept. 17km E of St Brieuc. 1.5km N of Lamballe in direction of Pleneuf-Val-Andre.
On site/nearby: toilets, shwrs, elec hook-ups.

50. Camping Manoir de Bonteville, Montours, 35460 Ille-et-Vilaine. M. Pierre MAUSSANT. Tel 02 99 95 16 60. 25 pitches. 37F. Easter-All Saints (11th Nov).
48km NE of Rennes. 14km NW of Fougeres, D978 twds St James. Bonteville is off to left in direction of Cogles.
On site/nearby: toilets, shwrs, elec hook-ups, laundry facilities, payphone, shop, rstrnt.

Foreign Fields

51. La Maison Neuve, 35490 Chauvigne. Marie-Armelle & Henri RAULT. Tel 02 99 95 05 64. 10 pitches. 36F. All year; reservation needed in winter. 33km NE of Rennes. From Rennes take N175 twds Antrain. At Romazy turn R for Chauvigne.On site/nearby: toilets, shwrs, elec hook-ups, laundry facilities, payphone, shop, rstrnt.

52. Le Lot a Rieux, 56350 Rieux. Renee LE VILLOUX. Tel 02 99 91 90 25. 13 pitches. 32F. 50km ESE of Vannes. On D114 7km S of Redon. On site/nearby: toilets, shwrs, shop, rstrnt.

53. Camping Saint-Georges, 49350 St-Georges-des-7-Voies. M. & Mme Paul LOISEAU. Tel/fax 02 41 57 94 76. 25 pitches. 30F. May-Sept. 21km ESE of Angers. On S side of Loire follow N751. Site is off to L after passing D55 to St-Mathurin.On site/nearby: toilets, shwrs, elec hook-ups.

54. Loire Country Holidays, Les Coteaux Du Chalet, 49260 Montreuil Bellay. Jean BUTTERFIELD. Tel 02 41 38 74 17; fax 02 41 50 92 83. 6 pitches. 50F. Booking essential. 11km SSW of Saumur. From Saumur take N147 to Montreuil Bellay, where follow signs to Centre Ville, then turn immediately L onto small road signed to Les Coteaux du Chalet. At T junction turn R and immediately L. Les C du C is in 1.5km.
On site/nearby: toilets, shwrs, elec hook-ups, laundry facilities.

55. La Guillonniere, 37360 Beaumont-la-Ronce. Madeleine GERNIER. Tel 02 47 24 42 83. 6 pitches. 25F inclusive of hook-up. All year. 20km N of Tours. On D766 twds Angers.
On site/nearby: toilets, shwrs, elec hook-ups, payphone, shop, rstrnt.

56. Camping a la Ferme, La Salle, 37220 Avon-les-Roches. Jocelyne & Remi DESBOURDES. Tel 02 47 95 24 30; fax 02 47 95 24 83. 6 pitches. 34F. Easter-All Saints (11th Nov). 40km ESE of Saumur. On D757, L'Ile Bouchard-Azay le Rideau. To E of road, 4km N of L'Ile B. On site/nearby: toilets, shwrs, elec hook-ups, rstrnt.

57. Camping Accueil a la Ferme, 37220 Panzoult. Guy & Yvette, Francois & Claude, CAILLE. Tel/fax 02 47 58 53 16. 15 pitches. 30F. May-Sept. 37km ESE of Saumur. On N bank of river Vienne, off D8, 12km ESE of Chinon. On site/nearby: toilets, shwrs, elec hook-ups.

58. Camping Le Ragis, 85300 Challans. M. & Mme Joseph GUYON. Tel/fax 02 51 68 08 49. 60 pitches. 73F. All year. 50km SSW of Nantes. From Challans take D32, after 2km turn R at top of an incline.
On site/nearby: toilets, shwrs, elec hook-ups, laundry facilities, payphone, shop, rstrnt.

59. La Rocaille, Les Barres, 85700 Pouzages. Peter & Jean GRANT. Tel 02 51 92 81 03. 6 pitches. 40F. All year. 75km SE of Nantes. 22km W of Bressuire, from where follow D960bis, bear R at St Mesmin. Les Barres in 4km. On site/nearby: toilets; laundry facilities and payphone by arrangement.

60. La Violliere, Breuil Barret, 85120 La Chataigneraie. Peter & Chris Woodman. Tel 02 51 87 44 82. 95km SE of Nantes. On D949 E from La Chataigneraie twds Poitiers, go through Breuil Barret, then 2nd R after railway bridge. On site/nearby: toilets, shwrs, rstrnt.

South West France

61. Domaine de Bois l'Abesse, 79340 Vasles. Nicole AUDOUIN. Tel 05 49 69 03 46. 8 pitches. 30F. Apr-Nov. 28km W of Poitiers. From Poitiers take N149 twds Parthenay. At Chalandray, turn L onto D321 to Vasles.
On site/nearby: toilets, shwrs, elec hook-ups, payphone, rstrnt.

62. Camping a la Ferme de la Raudiere, 86190 Latille. M. Francois GIRARD. Tel 05 49 54 81 36. 25 pitches. 30F. May-Sept. 22km WNW of Poitiers. From Poitiers take N149 twds Parthenay. At Vouille bear L onto D62 to Latille. On site/nearby: toilets, shwrs, elec hook-ups, laundry facilities, payphone, shop, rstrnt.

63. Le Moulin de Trenouillet, Route de Brioux, 79110 Chef-Boutonne. Christine & Tony MURLESS. Tel 05 49 29 77 38; tel/fax 05 49 29 73 46. 32 pitches. 54F-73F. All year. 60km SW of Poitiers. From the N10 50km S of Poitiers exit to D948 twds Niort. After 5km bear L at Sauze-Vassais onto D1 to Chef-Boutonne. Moulin de T is 2km to W of Chef-B on D740. On site/nearby: toilets, shwrs, elec hook-ups, laundry facilities, shop, rstrnt.

64. Le Peyrat 'Ecosse', 86750 Millac. Alan & Hilda JAMIESON. Tel 05 49 84 50 88. 6 pitches. 60F. All year. 65km NW of Linmoges; 22km N of Confolens, near L'Isle Jourdain. From centre of L'Isle J, 1.4km route Mouterre D28. On site/nearby: toilets, shwrs, elec hook-ups, laundry facilities, payphone, shop, rstrnt.

65. Aire Naturelle de Camping, 3 Bas Prezelle, 17120 Arces. M. Dominique ROY. Tel/fax 05 46 90 70 31. 25 pitches. 55F-63F. Easter-Oct. 85 km NNW of Bordeaux near E bank of river Gironde. Leave Royan to Lorignac coast road at Talmont by D114E for Arces. On site/nearby: toilets, shwrs, elec hook-ups, laundry facilities, payphone, rstrnt.

66. Les Moreaux, Virollet 17260, Par Gemozac. Richard & Lynn DAY. Tel 05 46 94 15 16. 5 pitches. 81km N of Bordeaux; 13km W of Pons. From exit 26 of Autoroute A10 take D732 twds Royan. 2km past Gemozac turn L onto D244 for Virollet. On site/nearby: shops.

67. Camping Chardon, Vallieres, 17800 Pons. M. TALBOT. 05 46 94 04 86. 21 pitches. 40F. Apr-Sept.
80km N of Bordeaux; 3km SW of Pons. From exit 26 of Autoroute A10 take D732 twds Pons. Then at 1km take
1st or 2nd road on R. On site/nearby: toilets, shwrs, elec hook-ups, payphone, rstrnt.

68. La Bujhollerie, 17500 Saint-Simon-de-Bordes. Colette CELLOU. Tel 05 46 48 05 21. 6 pitches. 57F including
electricity. May-Sept (avoid July & Aug). 63km NNE of Bordeaux. 3km S of Jonzac on D19.
On site/nearby: toilets, shwrs, elec hook-ups, laundry facilities, shop, rstrnt.

69. Camping a la Ferme de la Chassagne, 16240 Villefagnan. M. PELOQUIN. Tel 05 45 31 61 47; fax 05 45 29 55 87. 12
pitches. 54F. All year. 68km SSW of Poitiers; 8km WSW of Ruffec. From N10, exit at Ruffec. Take direction of Villefagnan
– 10km, then L onto D27. On site/nearby: toilets, shwrs, elec hook-ups, laundry facilities, payphone, shop, meals.

70. La Maison Rose, La Haute Terne, 16230 Luxe. Mrs Lesley KING. Tel 05 45 22 75 05 (or UK 0044 1622
752684). 6 pitches. 80F-100F. School holidays only. 27km N of Angouleme. 6km NW of Mansle direction Aigre.
After bridge over Charente turn R then 1st L up hill. At top turn L past water tower to pink house.
On site/nearby: toilets, shwrs, shop, rstrnt.

71. La Blanchie, 16270 Suris, Roumazieres-Loubert. Mrs. M. HARRIS. Tel/fax 05 45 89 33 19. 25 pitches. 60F. All
year.43km NE of Angouleme; 6km SE of Roumaziere-Loubert. Take N141 from Angouleme twds Limoge. After
Roumaziere-L at La Peruse turn R onto D52 to Suris.
On site/nearby: toilets, shwrs, elec hook-ups, payphone, shop, rstrnt.

72. Chateau Sipian, Vignobles Mehaye, 28 route du Porte de Goulee, 33340 Valeyrac. Mme & M. MEHAYE. Tel 05
56 41 56 05; fax 05 56 41 35 36. No charges. All year. 70km NNW of Bordeaux near W bank of river Gironde.
Take N215 N from Bordeaux to Lesparre-Medoc, then bear R onto D201 for 10km.
On site/nearby: Own sanitation essential.

73. Camping, 56 Route de Plassan, 33340 Lesparre-Medoc. Mrs. A. SHARMAN. Tel 05 56 73 42 22. 6 pitches.
58km NNW of Bordeaux. Take N215 N from Bordeaux to Lesparre-Medoc, then turn S twds Plassan.
On site/nearby: toilets, shwrs, shops.

74. Chateau Gerbaud, Clos Gerbaud, Saint Pey d'Armens. Mme Patricia FORGEAT-CHABROL. Tel 05 57 47 12
39/05 57 47 16 06 fax 05 55 70 47 20. 15 pitches. No charges. 36km E of Bordeaux; 12km SE of Liburne. On
D936 from Bordeaux, at St Pey d'Armens beside a tabac turn R twds Gerbaud St Terre for 200m, then 1st L.
On site/nearby: payphone, rstrnt, own sanitation essential.

75. Chateau Labutit, Vignobles Bouchard, 33490 Haut St-Maixant. Mme BOUCHARD. Tel 05 56 62 02 44 fax 05 56 62
09 46. 10/15 pitches. No charges. 38km SE of Bordeaux; 5km NNE of Langon. Leaving Langon take RN113 to east.
Leave it at 1st lights after crossing the Garonne; keep going twds Verdelais. After 2km from the exit follow signs for
Vignobles Bouchard. On site/nearby: toilets, payphone.

76. Le Grand Pre, route de Castelfaloux, 'Castagnoue', 33430 Bazas. Philippe de CHENERILLES. Tel 05 56 25 11
18; fax 05 56 25 90 52. 18 pitches. 70F-120F; 37F-62F small tents. May-Sept. 58km SE of Bordeaux; 16km SSE of
Langon. From Bazas head SE twds Casteljaloux (D655), then 2nd R after 1km.
On site/nearby: toilets, shwrs, elec hook-ups, laundry facilities, payphone, shop, rstrnt.

77. Camping de la Ripole, Route du Stade, 24300 Abjat S/Bandiat. Mme Regine JARRETON. Tel 05 53 56 86 85 or
05 53 56 38 81. 30 pitches. 50F. 46km ESE of Angouleme. 10km NE of Nontron by D78.
On site/nearby: toilets, shwrs, elec hook-ups, laundry facilities.

78. Camping Le Touroulet, St Jory de Chalais, 24800 Chaleix. Doris NORMAN. Tel 05 53 62 07 90. 45F.
60km ESE of Angouleme. 3km W of the N21 between Chalus and Thiviers. Take D98 through Chaleix. 1km past
Chaleix site is is signed to L, down hill opposite lake, on R. On site/nearby: toilets, shwrs, elec hook-ups, rstrnt.

79. Le Bois du Corderc, Le Gaunies, 24420 Antonne-et-Trigonant. Mme Kim WILKINSON. Tel 05 53 06 00 65
fax 05 53 05 99 48. 30 pitches. 40F. 12km ENE of Perigueux. From Perigueux take N21 twds Limoges. 1km past
Antonne-et-T turn R at Routier restaurant. Site is behind restrnt down dirt track into woods.
On site/nearby: toilets, shwrs, elec hook-ups, laundry facilities, payphone, rstrnt.

80. Home Farm, Guinet, 24610 Minzac. Jill JOINER. Tel 05 53 80 72 13; fax 05 53 81 68 95. 6 pitches. 65F. All year.
50km ENE of Bordeaux. From Libourne take N89 twds Perigueux. After 26km turn R onto D10 twds Villefranche-
de-Lonchat. Minzac is 4km. On site/nearby: elec hook-ups, payphone, shop, rstrnt; own sanitation essential.

81. Hamelin-Perigord-Vacances, 24290 St. Amand-de-Coly. M. HAMELIN. Tel 05 53 51 68 59 or 05 53 51 60 64 (fax).
55 pitches. 61F. Mid June-mid Sept. 44km ESE of Perigueux. From Perigueux go E on N89 twds Brive-la-
Gaillarde. At Le Lardin-St-Lazare bear R twds Souillac on D62. After 6km turn R to St-Amand de Coly.
On site/nearby: toilets, shwrs, elec hook-ups, laundry facilities, payphone, rstrnt.

*Foreign
Fields*

82. Le Grel, 24250 Domme. Derek & Doreen WILLIAMS (agents). Tel (UK) 0044 151 6088119 (or write: 4 Roman Road, Storeton, Wirral, L63 6HS, UK). 8 pitches. £7.50 (sterling). 58km SE of Perigueux. Domme is 10km S of Sarlat-la-Caneda on D46. On site/nearby: toilets, shwrs, elec hook-ups, laundry facilities, payphone, rstrnt.

83. Mirathon, 47120 Baleyssagues, Duras. Barbara GRAY & David AMY. Tel 05 53 83 08 47. 3 pitches for tents. 30F. 70km SW of Perigueux. From Ste-Foy-la-Grande go S on D708 to Duras. Just past Duras turn R onto D668, then R, L and R to Baleyssagues. On site/nearby: toilets, shwrs, laundry facilities.

84. Camping Moulin de Mandassagne, Parranquet, 47210 Villereal. Mme PIMOUGET. Tel/fax 05 53 36 04 02. 60 pitches. 45F. Apr-Oct. 53km NNE of Agen. Parranquet is 1km N of D104 between Vellereal and Monpazier. On site/nearby: toilets, shwrs, elec hook-ups, laundry facilities, payphone, shop, meals.

85. Camping Le Chateau, 40120 Bourriot-Bergonce. Mrs Margaret SPRINGETT. 05 58 93 36 22. 38F. All year. 86km SSE of Bordeaux. From Langon take D932 twds Roquefort for 44km, then bear L onto D24 through Bourriot-Bergonce to just other side of Bergonce. On site/nearby: toilets, shwrs, elec hook-ups, shop, rstrnt.

86. Rose d'Armagnac Camping, 32250 Montreal du Gers. Claire OWEN. Tel/fax 05 62 29 47 70 (or UK agent 0044 1489 582413). 13 pitches. £5 (sterling). Apr-Oct. 48km NW of Auch. From Montreal go twds Fources. Take 1st L after stadium twds Cornellian and follow signs. From Fources, 1st R before Montreal twds Sos and follow signs. On site/nearby: toilets, shwrs, elec hook-ups, payphone, shop, rstrnt.

87. Camping a la Ferme de Barrachin, 32700 Lectoure. Guy & Christiane ESPARBES. Tel 05 62 68 84 57 fax 05 62 68 97 32. 8 pitches. 43F. Apr-Nov; reservations during the winter. 37km NNE of Auch. From Lectoure take N21 twds Agen, then R onto D23 twds Miradoux for abt 4km. On site/nearby: toilets, shwrs, elec hook-ups, payphone, meals.

88. Camping La Pose, 65400 Estaing. Ginette BOUYRIE. Tel 05 62 97 43 10 or 05 62 97 10 11. 25 pitches. 32F. All year. 23km SSW of Lourdes. From Lourdes take N21 S. At Argeles-Gazost bear R onto D918. After 2km turn L onto D103. La Pose is 1km before Le Lac d'Estaing, abt 15 km from Argeles-G. On site/nearby: toilets, shwrs, elec hook-ups, payphone, rstrnt.

89. Camping les Tilleuls, Le Saussa, 65120 Gedre. M. & Mme Francois MILLET. Tel 05 62 92 48 92. 25 pitches. 44F. Mid June-20 Sept. 36km S of Lourdes. From Lourdes, take N21 S through Argeles-Gazost, then D921 through Pierrefitte, Luz and finally Gedre. 200m after church turn R twds twds the high ground. 440m after bridge, turn L, site is 50m on L, turning after 1st house. On site/nearby: toilets, shwrs, elec hook-ups, laundry facilities, rstrnt.

Southern France

90. Camping du Champ de Donne, Saint Palavy, 46110 Cavagnac. Marcel CHANTELOUBE. Tel 05 65 32 12 53. 10 pitches. 33. Apr-Oct. 66km NNE of Cahors between Brive-la-Gaillarde and Vayrac. Turn off D20 to E, 4km S of Turenne. On site/nearby: toilets, shwrs, elec hook-ups, shop, rstrnt.

91. Camping L'Occitan, Laubarede, Peyrusse-le-Roc, 12220 Montbazens. M. JOULIE. 05 65 80 43 32. 16 pitches. 30F. Mid June-mid Sept. 55km E of Cahors, in centre of triangle formed by Figeac, Decazeville and Villefranche-de-Rouergue, on D87 between Montbazens and Naussac. On site/nearby: toilets, shwrs, elec hook-ups, payphone.

92. Camping La Barette, Finiels, 48220 Le Pont-de-Montvert. Lucile & Almir PANTEL. Tel 04 66 45 81 82 or 04 66 45 82 16. 20 pitches. 50F. Mid June-mid Sept. 94km E of Rodez. 5km N of Le Pont-de-Montvert on D20. On site/nearby: toilets, shwrs, elec hook-ups, laundry facilities.

93. Camping de la Quillette, Rousses, 48400 Florac. Mme Alice ARGENSON. Tel 04 66 44 00 29. 25 pitches. 32F. Mid June-mid Sept. 81km ESE of Rodez; 14km S of Florac. From Florac, take N107 twds St Jean du Gard for 5.5km. Then turn R onto D907 twds Meyrueis. At Vanels turn L twds Rousses, St Jean du Gard, keeping on D907. On site/nearby: toilets, shwrs, payphone, rstrnt.

94. Camping La Garde, 48370 St Germain de Calberte, Randonnees en Cevennes. Cecile Bin PALAZON. Tel 04 66 45 94 82; fax 04 66 45 95 18. 60F-80F. 100km ESE of of Rodez. Between Florac and Ales, on D984, 8km S of N106. On site/nearby: toilets, shwrs, elec hook-ups, laundry facilities, payphone, shop.

95. La Camperie du Cande, 82240 Lapenche, Quercy. M. & Mme Lucien RENDIER. Tel 05 63 31 96 51. 6 pitches. 34F. May-Oct. 26km SSE of Cahors, between Cahors and Montauban. 5km from N20 and 6 km from Caussade on D103. La Camperie is just to the S of Lapenche on E side of river. On site/nearby: toilets, shwrs, elec hook-ups, payphone, shop, rstrnt.

96. Camping La Rigaudie, 81500 Giroussens. M. GABEN. Tel 05 63 41 67 20. 24 pitches. 50F. Apr-Nov. 33km NE of Toulouse. Leave Autoroute A 68 by exit 7 and take D631 to Giroussens. Site is about 2km to NE of Giroussens. On site/nearby: toilets, shwrs, elec hook-ups, laundry facilities, payphone.

Reference Section Southern France

97. Camping a la Ferme de Pelicon, 34150 Gignac. Isabelle & Baudouin THILLAYE DU BOULLAY. Tel/fax 04 67 57 68 92. 12 pitches. 36F. Mar-Nov. 27km W of Montpellier. On entering Gignac from Montpellier take 1st road on left (D111) for 3km. On site/nearby: toilets, shwrs, elec hook-ups, laundry facilities, payphone, shop, rstrnt.

98. Camping Domaine de Querelle, 34410 Serignan, Herault. Yolande & Jean Luc ABEL. Tel 04 67 32 03 01. 65F. June-Sept. 11km SE of Beziers. From Beziers take D64 twds Valras-Plage. Domaine de Q is off to L just after Serignan. On site/nearby: toilets, shwrs, elec hook-ups, payphone, shop, rstrnt.

99. Camping a la Ferme de Preville, Route d'Auch, 31350 . M. PERISSAS. Tel/fax 05 61 88 23 12. 10 pitches. Apr-Oct. 50km ENE of Tarbes. Site is about 3km to NE of Boulogne S/Gesse on D632. On site/nearby: toilets, shwrs, elec hook-ups, payphone, shop, meals.

100. Camping les Asphodeles, Col du Portet d'Aspet, 3116 Portet d'Aspet. M. Joel EAMBON. Tel 05 61 96 13 16. 25 pitches. 40F. June-Sept. 72km SE of Tarbes. From St Gaudens on N117, take D5 S to Aspet. Continue through Aspet to Col du Portet d'Aspet. On site/nearby: toilets, shwrs, elec hook-ups, rstrnt.

101. Le Cathare, Chateau de la Barthe, 11410 Belflou. Mme CAZANAVE. Tel 04 68 60 32 49; fax 04 68 60 37 90. 25 pitches. 41F. May-Nov. 46km WNW of Carcassonne. Leave Autoroute A61 at Castelnaudary or Villefranche-de-Lauragais. Go via D624 or D625 to Salles-s-l'Hers and follow signs. On site/nearby: toilets, shwrs, elec hook-ups, laundry facilities, payphone, shop, rstrnt.

102. La Chevaline, 11270 Fanjeaux. H VAN DIJK. Tel 04 68 24 75 33. 10 pitches. 48F. Mid Apr-mid Oct. 26km W of Carcassonne. Leave Autoroute A61 at Bram, go twds Foix. Site is 9km from exit just past Fanjeaux. On site/nearby: toilets, shwrs, elec hook-ups, laundry facilities, payphone, shop, rstrnt.

103. Camping La Bastide de Madame, Route de Limoux, 11090 Carcassonne. Jean AUGE. Tel 04 68 26 80 06; fax 04 68 26 91 65. 25 pitches. 65F. July & Aug. 5km SW of Carcassonne. Leave Autoroute A61 at Carcassone West and take D118 twds Limoux. Turn R to site just after passing under railway bridge. On site/nearby: toilets, shwrs, elec hook-ups, laundry facilities, payphone.

104. Camping Val d'Aleth, 11580 Alet Les Bains. Mrs Christine CRANMER. Tel/fax 04 68 69 90 40. 37 pitches. 52F. All year. 26km SSW of Carcassonne. Leave Autoroute A61 at Carcassone West and take D118 twds Limoux. Site is 8km S of Limoux in Alet Les Bains on banks of River Aude. On site/nearby: toilets, shwrs, elec hook-ups, payphone, shop, rstrnt.

105. Camping Mas Gaillac, 09100 Bezac. M. & Mme Andre DELAVAULT. Tel 05 61 67 14 54. 8-10 pitches. 36F-50F. June-Sept. 63km WSW of Carcassonne. Take N20 to Pamiers, then N119 twds St Girons. Site is 4km to W of Pamiers twds Escosse. On site/nearby: toilets, shwrs, elec hook-ups.

South East France

106. Ferme Equestre, Malafretaz, 013340 Malafretaz. Josette CRETIN. Tel/fax 04 74 30 81 19. 6 pitches. 22F including electricity. 25km E of Macon. Leave Autoroute A40 at exit 3. Take D28 through Bage-le-Chatel and Montrevel-en-Bresse to Malafretaz. On site/nearby: toilets, shwrs, elec hook-ups, payphone, meals.

107. Camping Rural, Le Potay, 01370 Meillonas. Maurice JACQUET. Tel 04 74 51 31 95. 7 pitches. 27F. All year. 40km E of Macon. Leave Autoroute A40 at exit 6. Follow D52f E through Mangettes and Les Tupinieres to Meillonnas. On site/nearby: toilets, shwrs, elec hook-ups.

108. L'Ermitage des Clouz, Les Clouz, Vinzier, 74500 Evian-les-Bains. Jean SCHMITT. Tel 04 50 73 60 66/04 50 70 26 22. 6 pitches. 60F. 39km NE of Geneve. 13km by road from Thonon-les-Bains or Evian-les-Bains. On site/nearby: toilets, shwrs, elec hook-ups, laundry facilities, payphone, rstrnt.

109. Le Trepu, St Franc, 73360 Les Echelles. Marie Agnes & Jean CURTET-HOORNAERT. Tel 04 76 31 10 57. 12 pitches. 30F. Apr-Oct. 78km ESE of Lyons. St Franc is on junction of D38 and D39 about 2km to E of N6, 17km SW of Chambery. On site/nearby: toilets, shwrs, elec hook-ups, payphone, rstrnt.

110. Les Parauds, 07000 Flaviac. Paul MONTEIL. Tel 04 75 65 74 11. 6 pitches. 40F. May-Oct. 27km SSW of Valence. Leave Autoroute A7 to join N304 going twds Privas. Continue on N104. Site is at Flaviac, 6km before Privas, on farm by edge of river. On site/nearby: toilets, shwrs, elec hook-ups, payphone, shop, rstrnt.

111. Les Marroniers, 07110 Montreal. Sebastien JAUZION. Tel/fax 04 75 36 82 54. 25 pitches. 34F. Apr-Sept. 36km W of Montelimar. On D104, 13km SSW of Aubenas, turn onto D5 twds Largentiere. Just before Largentiere, after going under viaduct, turn L onto D212 twds Montreal and Laurac. Just before Montreal bear L to Les Marroniers. On site/nearby: toilets, shwrs, elec hook-ups, laundry facilities, payphone, shop, meals.

112. Camping de la Falaise, 07120 Baluzac. M. BERRE. Tel 04 75 37 74 27. 20 pitches. 60F. 30km W of Montelimar. On N102, 8km SE of Aubenas, turn S onto D103. At Vogue bear L onto D579, then R onto D294 to Baluzac. On site/nearby: toilets, shwrs, elec hook-ups, laundry facilities, payphone, shop, rstrnt.

Foreign Fields

113. Chevrieres, 26450 Roynac. Andre GILLES. Tel/fax 04 75 90 11 18. 6 pitches. 29F. Easter-Oct. 18km NE of Montelimar. Leave Autoroute A7 to join N304 and then D104 twds Crest and Gap. At Crest turn S onto D538 twds Montelimar. At Puys St Martin turn R onto D107 to Roynac. On site/nearby: toilets, shwrs, elec hook-ups, laundry facilities, rstrnt.

114. Camping a la Ferme, Lochette, 26150 Pontaix. Elie ROURY. Tel 04 75 21 22 14. 10 pitches. 23F. June-Sept. 36km SE of Valence. Leave Autoroute A7 to join N304 and then D104 twds Crest and Gap. Pontaix is about 25km after Crest. On site/nearby: toilets, shwrs, elec hook-ups, laundry facilities, shop, rstrnt.

115. Le Moulin de Cost, 26170 Buis Les Baronnies. Michel CHASSAGNAC. Tel 04 75 28 09 82; fax 04 75 28 08 23. 30 pitches. 50F. Mid Apr-Sept. 40km ENE of Orange. From Carpentras to the SE of Orange, take D938 N twds Nyons. 3km after Malaucene turn R onto D13 and continue on D5 twds Buis Les Baronnies. Site is 3km before Buis Les B, off to R on bank of river. On site/nearby: toilets, shwrs, elec hook-ups, laundry facilities, payphone, shop, rstrnt.

116. Camping de Monteglin, 26 Avenue de Monteglin, 05300 Laragne-Monteglin. M. Auguste TRUPHEME. Tel 04 92 65 02 94/04 92 65 06 24 fax 04 92 65 00 76. 50 pitches. 45F. 33km SW of Gap. From Gap take N85 S twds Marseilles. After 23km, at Monetier-Allemont, join D942 to Laragne-Monteglin. Site is on outskirts of Laragne-M. On site/nearby: toilets, shwrs, elec hook-ups, laundry facilities, payphone, shop, rstrnt.

117. Camping Belle-Vue, 84410 Crillon-Le-Brave. M. & Mme Yves MASCLAUX. Tel 04 90 62 42 29; fax 04 90 62 34 55. 25 pitches. 62F. March-Oct. 27km E of Orange. From Carpentras to the SE of Orange, take D974 NE twds Bedouin. After 11km, just past turning to Crillon-Le-Brave, turn right to site. On site/nearby: toilets, shwrs, elec hook-ups, laundry facilities, payphone.

118. Camping Les Jonquiers, 84750 St Martin-de-Castillon. M. Henri MANGEOT. Tel 04 90 75 20 11; fax 04 90 75 25 49 or 04 90 75 12 44. 25 pitches. 45F. Apr-Sept. 37km N of Aix-en-Provence. On N100, about 6km to E of Apt, turn L onto D48 twds St Martin-de-Castillon. Site is a little before the village. On site/nearby: toilets, shwrs, elec hook-ups, payphone, rstrnt.

119. Camping des Mouquets, Castellet, 14400 Apt. Raymonde BOUSEOULE. Tel 04 90 75 28 62/04 90 75 28 62. 10 pitches. 60F. 35km N of Aix-en-Provence. On N100, about 9km to E of Apt, turn S to Castellet. On site/nearby: toilets, shwrs, elec hook-ups, payphone.

120. Ferme de Vauveniere, 04410 Saint-Jurs. Helene SAUVANE. Tel/fax 04 92 74 44 18. 25 pitches. 40F. Apr-Sept. 74km NW of Cannes (measured from exit 42 of Autoroute A8). St-Jurs is 4km to N of northernmost tip of D952 between Castellane and Greoux-les-Bains. From Riez on D952, take D953 to N. 1km after Puimoisson bear R onto D108 for St-Jurs. On site/nearby: toilets, shwrs, elec hook-ups, laundry facilities, payphone.

121. Camping a la Ferme, Vignobles des Hautes Collines, 800 Chemin des Sausses, 06640 Saint-Jeannet. M. Georges-Denis RASSE. Tel/fax 04 93 24 96 01. 75 pitches. 50F. Apr-Oct. 10km WNW of Nice. Exit from Autoroute A8 at Cagnes-sur-Mer. Go twds La Gaude and St Jeannet – 12km. On site/nearby: toilets, shwrs, elec hook-ups.

122. Les Amandaies, 13890 Mouries. M. & Mme Francis CROUAU. Tel/fax 04 90 47 50 59 fax 04 90 47 61 79. 6 pitches. 60F. June-10 Nov. 23km E of Arles. From Arles take D17 twds Salon-de-Provence. After Murie and junction with D5, turn R onto minor road. The farm is at the end of this road after 2km. On site/nearby: toilets, shwrs, elec hook-ups, payphone, shop, rstrnt.

STOP PRESS • STOP PRESS • STOP PRESS • STOP PRESS • STOP PRESS • STOP PRESS • STOP PRESS

123. Le Cator, 32420 Simorre. Beate FORDERER. Tel 05 62 65 33 44; fax 05 62 65 30 99. 6 pitches. 46.50F. All year 60km WSW of Toulouse. From Toulouse take D124 through L'Isle Jourdain twds Auch. On leaving Gimont turn L onto D12 through Saramon to Simorre. On site/nearby: toilets, shwrs, elec hook-ups, laundry facilities, meals.

124. La Lande, 53380 La Croixille. Alexandre & Odette JARRY. Tel 02 43 68 57 00. 6 pitches. 26F. Apr-Oct. 50km ENE of Rennes. From Vitre to E of Rennes take D777 twds Ernee. At La Croixille turn R onto minor road. La Lande is about halfway along this road before reaching the D208 running between Juvigne and Le Bourgneuf La Foret. On site/nearby: toilets, shwrs, elec hook-ups, shop, rstrnt.

125. Camping le Ronquet, 55 Chaniere du Commerce, 50230 Agon-Coutainville. M. Maurice VINCENT. Tel 02 33 47 05 29. 25 pitches. 52F. June-Aug. 38km WSW of St Lo; 12km W of Coutances. On site/nearby: toilets, shwrs, elec hook-ups.

126. Camping Vezins, Le Jardin, Vezins, 50540 Isigny-le-Buat. Mr K. NUTT. Tel 02 33 48 25 83. 12 pitches. 45F. All year. 25km N of Fougeres. Site is 4km to S of N176 between St Hilaire-de-Harcouet and Ducey. Take D582 S'wards twds St Laurent de Ter. Then fork L onto D565E through Le Bourg. Site is on L. On site/nearby: toilets, shwrs, elec hook-ups, payphone, meals, shop.

127. Camping La Roquette, Quartier Les Basses Roques, 83520 Roquebrune-sur-Argens. Rene & Yvonne BLANC. Tel/fax 04 94 45 78 61. 8km W of Frejus. Leave Autoroute A8 or N7 at Le Muy. Then follow arrowed route to Roquebrune-sur-A. On site/nearby: toilets, shwrs, elec hook-ups, laundry facilities, payphone.

Travelling from (or via) England? The following companies can help you get across (or under) the Channel!

P&O European Ferries
Tel: 0990 980980
Fax: 01304 223464

Dover-Calais
Portsmouth-Le Havre
Portsmouth-Cherbourg

North Sea Ferries
Tel: 0148 377177
Fax: 01428 706438

Hull-Zeebrugge

Stena Line
Tel: 0990 707070
Fax: 01233 202361

Dover-Calais
Newhaven-Dieppe
Southampton-Cherbourg

Brittany Ferries
Tel: 0990 360360
Fax: 01705 873237

Portsmouth-Caen
Portsmouth-St Malo
Poole-Cherbourg
Poole-St Malo
Plymouth-Roscoff

Sea France
Tel: 01304 212696
Fax: 01304 240033

Dover-Calais

Hoverspeed
Tel: 01304 240241
Fax: 01304 240088

Dover-Calais
Folkestone-Boulogne

Sally Ferries
Tel: 0990 595522
Fax: 01834 589329

Ramsgate-Dunkirk

Le Shuttle
Tel: 0990 353535

Folkestone-Calais via
Channel Tunnel

Foreign Fields

HAUTE CUISINE A LA SUPERMARKET

Let us assume for the purposes of this article that at some stage in your travels you will relinquish the restaurants and abandon the brasseries for long enough to contemplate preparing the odd meal for yourself. And that this (not necessarily sound) idea is accompanied by a desire to enjoy the experience. In France, happily, this is gloriously possible – almost certainly, inevitable. For in France a quick rummage round a supermarket and five minutes over a gas ring can produce food to impress the most discerning. Particularly those among the discerning who don't know what comes in a tin and what doesn't.

DON'T EVEN THINK ABOUT trying to reproduce the sort of food you have at home. You won't be able to, unless you want to spend your holidays searching for unobtainable ingredients, and even if you succeed it'll feel like work. Vow to eat nothing you'd eat at home and every meal becomes an experience. Make this the time, for example, you try snails and frogs' legs. Buy snails ready-stuffed with garlic butter in the frozen food department. Frozen frogs' legs come in bags – sprinkle them with powdered garlic (herbs and spices department) and gently fry them. You may hate them, but you'll hate them with authority.

Rummage around the tins of made-up meat dishes. Try cassoulet, a sort of hearty bean stew with lots of bacon, sausage and bits of goose. A Danish friend told me the Vikings ate something similar before setting off across icy seas; it does seem a bit incongruous in its native, near-Mediterranean Toulouse, but it tastes wonderful. Also good are navarin of lamb, sausages with black lentils, potée de choux and about forty other gourmet delights needing no more than a can opener and a nonchalant shrug (practise this).

Don't despise the tinned veg. In France they are an art form; there are things here in cans you didn't know existed in the wild. Try flageolets (I always thought these were Elizabethan musical instruments), petits pois with tiny onions and scraps of lettuce leaf, celery hearts, French beans – the essential key, though, to buying them is to understand the class system that pertains. They come in different qualities – look for 'extra fin' on the label and you'll get the best.

At the meat counter, be daring. Try sanglier (wild boar), veal if you don't have conscientious objections, horse if you must. Cotes de porc (big pork chops) are cheap and flavoursome; lamb is usually expensive but comes in some ingenious shapes and sizes with much string and fancy bits, good for impressing people. The French butcher beef in baffling ways, with steaks cut 'across the grain'; they'll mince any piece you choose for you, though, ready for you to add sauce over which you've slaved for hours or, alternatively, poured out of a jar.

Find a supermarket big enough to have a large fish counter. Everything will be fresh – a fishmonger I know in Brittany throws away anything not sold by lunchtime and starts again when the next catch comes in. Lobsters and crabs on the hoof we're used to – beware though all those cockle and clam type creatures. They're usually sold raw, and very much alive and chomping; fingers can be lost. Treat winkles with caution, too – it can be disconcerting to have a small wormy creature pop its head out to look at you just as you're preparing your pin. Fish soup in great glass jars is wonderful, as is 'surimi' if they have it – a sort of coleslaw made with fish sticks.

Buy your bread in a supermarket only if you must. Infinitely better to cycle to the local boulangerie in the early morning for it. What you should buy in the supermarket is one of the long thin bags the French make to CARRY it in. Anyone who's ever carried a bare baguette on a bike will know why.

With dairy products, timing is everything. Mercifully, the French seem to be more interested these days in fresh milk; unless you like the long-life stuff which they still sell in huge quantities, look for plastic bottles of 'lait frais entier' or 'lait frais demi-ecremé', semi-skimmed. Hundreds of cheeses to choose from, of course – more now, I suspect, than General de Gaulle's much-quoted 265 – the secret is buying them just when they're ready to eat, a feat of timing taken very, very seriously in France. I recall trying to buy a Camembert once; having responded to the vendor's question by saying it was to eat that same evening, he refused to sell me one, saying that none of his were ready. If you can see its brown rind through its wax paper packaging, a Camembert is ready for consumption. Cheese marked 'lait cru' is made with unpasteurised milk and ripens with astonishing enthusiasm left out of the fridge; catch it before it creeps out of the door and it'll taste sublime. Fromage à la supermarket compares very favourably with 'fromage à la ferme', which often tastes of very little (particularly the little round ones endearingly called crottins – 'goats' droppings').

Abandon all thoughts of 'regime' ('diet', in France more an abstract concept than a fact of anyone's life) when approaching the patisserie. French tarts, friend Maurice told me, are the best in the world. So are French nuns – little cottage-loaf confections of choux pastry and calories called 'religieuses'. Even the paving-slab-like 'flan' tastes divine. For campers and caravanners with little space, limited cooking facilities and unpredictable itineraries, all manner of goodies lurk on the shelves. French packet soups are excellent; try 'gratinée', traditional onion soup. (To be truly traditional, float toasted slices of baguette on top, then sprinkle with grated cheese and grill lightly; the early-morning porters in the Paris markets invented this as a winter breakfast dish). Sneak a few packet sauce mixes into your trolley; a sachet of 'sauce au poivre' turns pork chops into something seriously Gallic. Little tins of fish in various sauces (mackerel in mustard, for example), big tins of paella, even whole chickens in tins – there are endless possibilities, and endless fun to be had searching for them!

Real
Exploring

Essential Vocab

A campsite	Un terrain de camping
A pitch	Un emplacement
A tent	Une tente
A caravan	Une caravane
A motor caravan	Un camping car
An awning	Un auvent
A car	Une voiture
A motorbike	Une moto
A bike	Un vélo
One night	Une nuit
A week	Une semaine
A person	Une personne
An adult	Un adulte
A child	Un enfant
An electric hook-up	Un branchement électrique

The toilets	Les toilettes
The toilet/washing block	Le bloc sanitaire
A shower	Une douche
The dustbins	Les poubelles
A washing machine	Une machine á laver
A tumble drier	Un séche-linge
Drinking water	Eau potable
Reception	La réception
Swimming pool	La piscine
In the sun	Au soleil
In the shade	A l'ombre
The proprietor	Le propriétaire
To book	Réserver
To arrive	Arriver
To stay	Rester
To leave	Partir
To pay	Régler
To come back	Revenir

– and that most useful French word of all – un truc, which means 'a thingy'!

Foreign Fields

Real

Exploring **FUN ON THE WAY**

Exploring a country comes to life when you understand a little of its past. See how much you know of what made France the way it is.

1. Who painted the walls of the Lascaux caves? Where are they?

2. What ancient relics can be seen at Carnac in Brittany?

3. Who called Provence 'Provincia'?

4. Where did the Vandals come from?

5. Who defeated the Romans and became King of France?

6. Where would you find the Normans' close cousins?

7. In which French city did the Pope once reside? Where is it?

8. In what year was the battle of Agincourt fought? And where is Agincourt?

9. Who was the Maid of Orleans? Where is Orleans?

10. How long did the Hundred Years' War last?

11. Who did the Edict of Nantes set out to protect? Where's Nantes?

12. Who was the Sun King – and where did he live?

13. Who said, "I think, therefore I am"?

14. What happened on 14 July 1789? And where?

15. Who was responsible for The Terror?

16. Where was Napoléon Bonaparte born? Where did he die?

17. What is the 'Code Napoléon'?

18. Who was the last King of France? And when?

19. What started in 1870?

20. What was the Dreyfus Affair about? Who said "J'accuse...."?

21. For what event was the Eiffel Tower built?

22. What was signed in 1919?

23. Which regions did France win back after World War 1?

24. Where was the Maginot Line? Why didn't it work?

25. What was the 'Maquis'?

26. Who said "Nobody can unite a country which has 265 kinds of cheese"?

27. What was the date of D-Day?

28. To what did De Gaulle say "Non"?

29. What happened in Paris in 1968?

30. Who was elected President in 1981? On what date did he die?

31. Who is now the President?

32. What are the 'Académie Francaise' and the 'Comédie Francaise'?

33. When did the Channel tunnel open?

34. What is Minitel?

35. In which year did production of the 2CV car cease?